Power Maths

Year 6 Textl

Series Editor: Tony Staneff

Flo

Flo is flexible.

She looks for different ways to solve a problem.

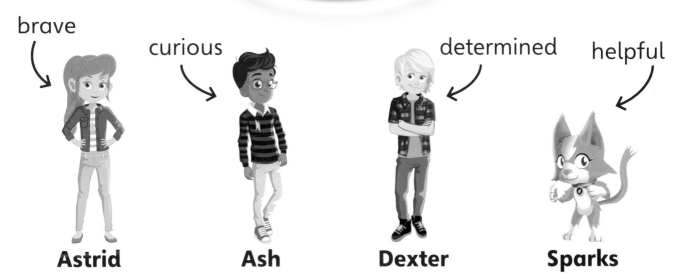

brave

curious

determined

helpful

Astrid

Ash

Dexter

Sparks

Pearson

Contents

This tells you which page you need.

I can't wait to begin!

How to use this book

These pages make sure we're ready for the unit ahead. Find out what we'll be learning and brush up on your skills!

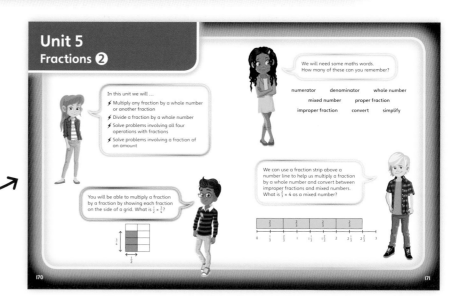

Discover

Lessons start with **Discover**.

Here, we explore new maths problems.

Can you work out how to find the answer?

Don't be afraid to make mistakes. Learn from them and try again!

Share

Next, we share our ideas with the class.

Did we all solve the problems the same way?
What ideas can you try?

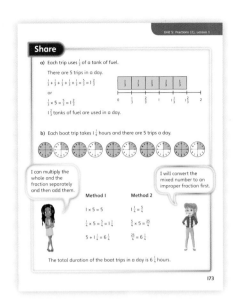

Think together

Then we have a go at some more problems together.
Use what you have just learnt to help you.

We'll try a challenge too!

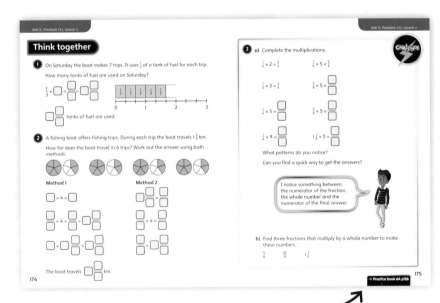

This tells you which page to go to in your **Practice Book**.

At the end of each unit there's an **End of unit check**. This is our chance to show how much we have learnt.

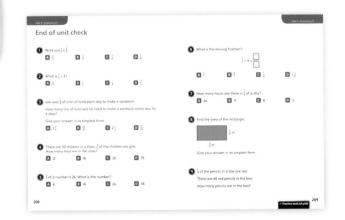

Unit 1
Place value within 10,000,000

In this unit we will …

- ⚡ Learn to read and write numbers to 10,000,000
- ⚡ Partition, compare and order numbers up to 10,000,000
- ⚡ Round numbers
- ⚡ Work with negative numbers

Do you remember what this is called? We will use it to help identify the place value of digits in a number.

M	HTh	TTh	Th	H	T	O
1	0	0	0	0	0	0

We will need some maths words. Can you explain the words you have met before?

ten thousands (10,000s)

hundred thousands (100,000s)

millions (1,000,000s)   ten million (10,000,000)

place value   partition   interval

estimate   compare   order

rounding   negative   positive

We will use this too! Can you find what the unlabelled values are?

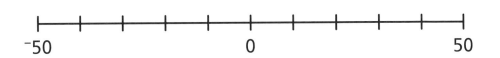

-50   0   50

Numbers to 1,000,000

Discover

I have made a 6-digit number using the cards. It has 4 hundreds.

My number has 2 ten thousands.

It is less than 800,000 and odd.

10,000 more than the number I have made is 106,287.

Richard

Lexi

2 4 6 7 8 9

1 **a)** What numbers could Richard have made using the digit cards shown?

How many different answers can you find?

b) What number has Lexi made?

8

Share

a)

I have made a 6-digit number using the cards. It has 4 hundreds.

HTh	TTh	Th	H	T	O
			4		

Put the 4 in the hundreds column.

My number has 2 ten thousands.

HTh	TTh	Th	H	T	O
	2		4		

Put the 2 in the ten thousands column.

It is less than 800,000 and odd.

The digit in the hundred thousands column must be less than 8.

The 7 or the 9 must go in the ones column to make the number odd.

HTh	TTh	Th	H	T	O
6	2		4		9

The digits that are left can be placed in either the thousands or the tens column. So Richard could have made:

627,489   726,489   629,487

628,479   728,469   628,497

I made 726,489 and 728,469 when I used 7 instead of 6 as the first digit.

I made 629,487 and 628,497 when I used 7 instead of 9 in the ones column.

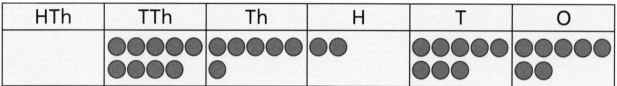

I represented 106,287 with counters on a place value grid, and then subtracted 10,000.

b) To find the number Lexi has made we need to work out what is 10,000 less than 106,287.

HTh	TTh	Th	H	T	O
	●●●●● ●●●●	●●●●● ●	●●		●●●●● ●●●	●●●●● ●●

Lexi has made the number 96,287.

Think together

1 Richard has made some numbers using different representations.

Say each number out loud. Then write each number in words.

3	2	5	6	7

HTh	TTh	Th	H	T	O
4	9	1	0	6	2

HTh	TTh	Th	H	T	O
●●	●●●●● ●●●●	●●●●●			

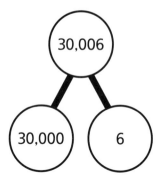

2 What is the value of the digit 5 in each of these numbers?

a)

TTh	Th	H	T	O
5	2	1	8	0

b)

HTh	TTh	Th	H	T	O
4	1	2	1	0	5

c) 26,515

d) 519,822

> Saying the numbers out loud helps me to understand the place value of each number.

---

3 Lexi makes a new number using these digit cards.

 CHALLENGE

| 0 | 1 | 2 | 4 | 8 | 9 |

She draws an arrow where her number is on the number line.

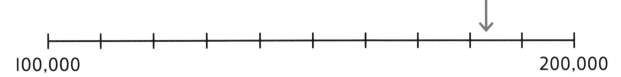

100,000   200,000

What number do you think Lexi has made?

> I can see the number line is split into 10 equal parts. This will help me to work out what the missing values are.

11

Numbers to 10,000,000 ①

Discover

① **a)** The comic books sold for one million pounds.

How many 100,000s are in one million?

b) Write the sale prices of the painting and the clock on place value grids.

Use the grids to help you to say the numbers out loud.

Share

a)

I used a number line to help me count up in 100,000s until I got to one million.

+100,000 +100,000 +100,000 +100,000 +100,000 +100,000 +100,000 +100,000 +100,000 +100,000

0 100,000 200,000 300,000 400,000 500,000 600,000 700,000 800,000 900,000 1,000,000

There are ten 100,000s in one million.

b)

M	HTh	TTh	Th	H	T	O
4	5	9	0	1	2	4

£4,590,124

The painting cost four million, five hundred and ninety thousand, one hundred and twenty-four pounds.

M	HTh	TTh	Th	H	T	O
	2	3	4	5	0	0

£234,500

The clock cost two hundred and thirty-four thousand, five hundred pounds.

Think together

1 A statue sells for £1,200,000.

How many 100,000s are there in 1,200,000?

£1,200,000

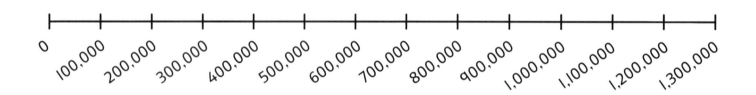

0   100,000   200,000   300,000   400,000   500,000   600,000   700,000   800,000   900,000   1,000,000   1,100,000   1,200,000   1,300,000

2 What numbers are shown in the place value grids?

Write your answers in numerals and in words.

a)

M	HTh	TTh	Th	H	T	O
	100,000 100,000 100,000 100,000	10,000 10,000 10,000 10,000 10,000 10,000	1,000 1,000	100 100 100		1 1 1 1 1

b)

M	HTh	TTh	Th	H	T	O
1,000,000 1,000,000 1,000,000 1,000,000 1,000,000	100,000		1,000 1,000 1,000 1,000	100 100 100		1 1 1 1 1 1 1 1 1

3 Lee is making numbers using counters on a place value grid.

Lee has 12 counters.

M	HTh	TTh	Th	H	T	O
●●	●●●●	●	●	●●●		●

a) What number has Lee made?

b) Which of the following numbers can Lee make using all 12 counters?

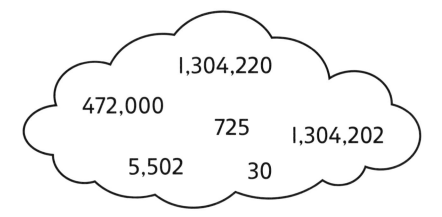

1,304,220

472,000

725

1,304,202

5,502

30

I wonder if there is a way of working out whether a number uses 12 counters.

I will try adding the digits together to see if that always works.

15

→ Practice book 6A p9

Numbers to 10,000,000 ②

Discover

Aki

Jamie

1 **a)** In the game, how much money does Jamie have?

b) How much money does Aki have?

Share

I used a place value grid to help me organise the numbers.

a)

M	HTh	TTh	Th	H	T	O
£1,000,000	£100,000	£10,000		£100	£10	£1
£1,000,000	£100,000	£10,000			£10	£1
£1,000,000	£100,000					£1
£1,000,000	£100,000					
	£100,000					

$$4,000,000 + 500,000 + 20,000 + 100 + 20 + 3 = 4,520,123$$

Jamie has £4,520,123.

b)

M	HTh	TTh	Th	H	T	O
£1,000,000		£10,000	£1,000			
£1,000,000		£10,000	£1,000			
		£10,000	£1,000			
		£10,000	£1,000			
		£10,000	£1,000			
		£10,000	£1,000			
			£1,000			
			£1,000			
			£1,000			
			£1,000			
			£1,000			
			£1,000			
2	0	6̸ 7	1̸ 1	0	0	0

Aki has £2,071,000.

I know that 10 thousands are equal to 1 ten thousand.

Think together

1 Andy and Reena join Jamie and Aki's game.

The place value grid shows Andy's money. How much money does he have?

M	HTh	TTh	Th	H	T	O
	£100,000 £100,000	£10,000 £10,000 £10,000 £10,000 £10,000 £10,000 £10,000	£1,000 £1,000 £1,000 £1,000 £1,000 £1,000	£100 £100 £100		£1 £1
0	2	7	6	3	0	2

200,000 + 70,000 + 6,000 + 300 + 2 = ☐

2 a) Find the missing numbers in this part-whole model.

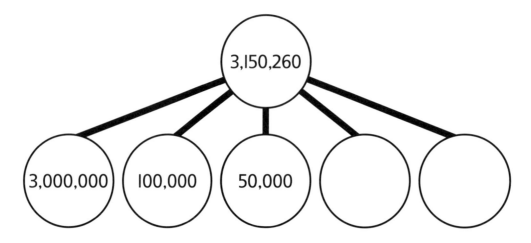

b) Draw a part-whole model for 706,053.

3 Write each of these partitioned numbers in numerals.

> 7,000,000 + 600,000 + 90,000 + 1,000 + 700 + 10 + 2

> 500,000 + 70,000 + 200 + 9

> 3,000,000 + 40,000 + 7,000 + 30 + 9

> 4,000,000 + 38,000 + 200

> 9,000 + 50,000 + 700,000 + 400 + 20 + 1

> four millions, three hundred thousands, nine hundreds, one ten and six ones

> 300,000 + 90,000 + 9,000 + 710

I am going to write the numbers in a place value grid to help me organise my work.

I do not think I need to use one.

19

→ Practice book 6A p12

Number line to 10,000,000

Discover

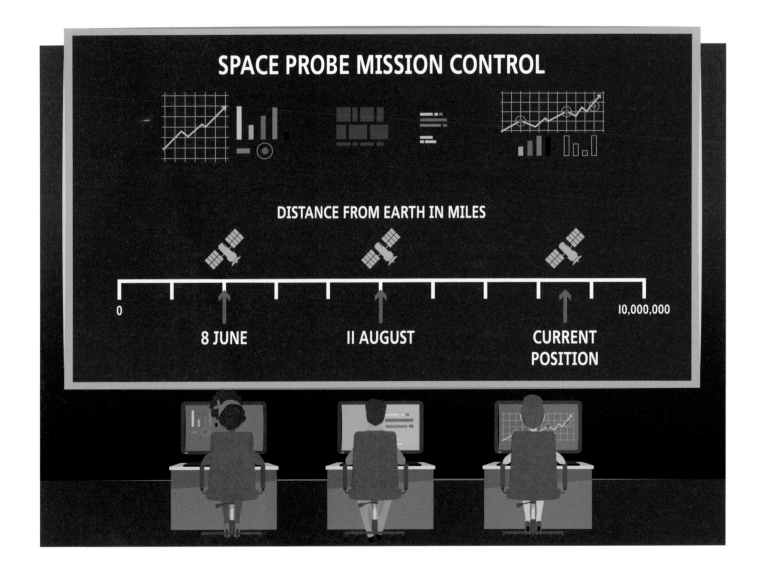

1) a) How far away from Earth is the space probe currently?

How accurate is your answer?

b) How far did the space probe travel between 8 June and 11 August?

Share

a)

> I know the line goes from 0 to 10,000,000 in 10 equal intervals, so each interval must be 1,000,000.

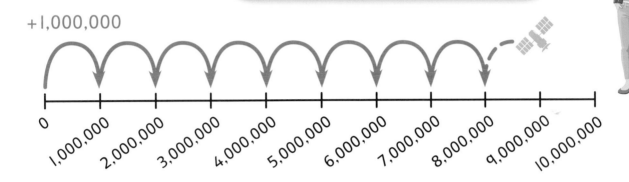

The probe is currently about half-way between 8,000,000 and 9,000,000.

The probe is approximately 8,500,000 miles from Earth.

Because the scale is quite small, we do not know if it is exactly half-way between these numbers.

> I had to think about the size of the scale. 1,000,000 is a lot to fit in one interval of the number line!

b) On 8 June, the space probe was 2,000,000 miles from Earth.

On 11 August, it was 5,000,000 miles from Earth.

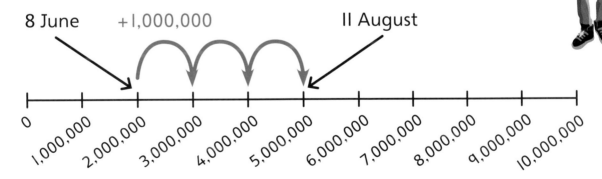

The probe travelled 3,000,000 miles between 8 June and 11 August.

Think together

1 Another probe is sent into space. The number line shows its distance from Earth.

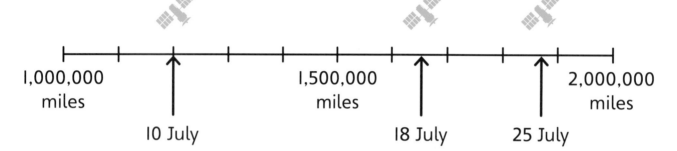

How far was the probe away from Earth on each date shown?

On 10 July, the probe was ⬜ miles from Earth.

On 18 July, it was ⬜ miles from Earth.

On 25 July, it was ⬜ miles from Earth.

> I think I can only estimate some of these answers.

2 The number lines show distance in miles. How many miles have these six space probes (A to F) travelled?

a)

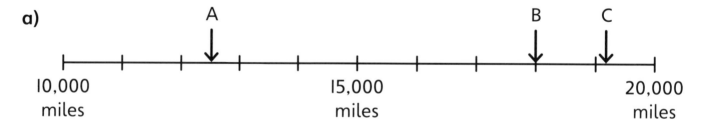

b)

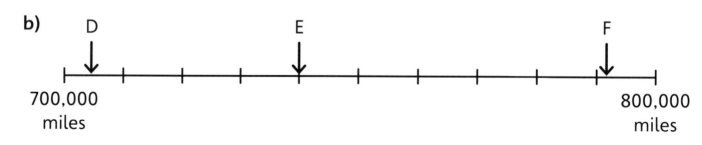

3 **a)** Kate says this arrow is pointing to 265,000.

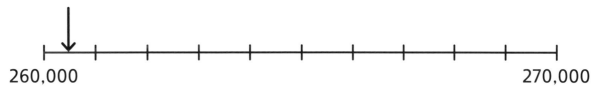

260,000   270,000

What mistake has Kate made?

b) Estimate the position of each arrow on this number line.

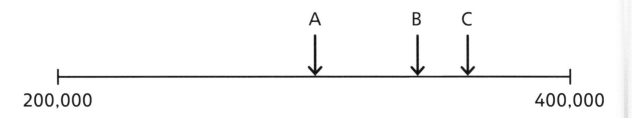

A   B   C

200,000   400,000

c) Where do you think 370,211 is on the number line?

I will try dividing the number line into equal parts.

I wonder whether I can show 370,211 accurately.

23

→ **Practice book 6A p15**

Comparing and ordering numbers to 10,000,000

Discover

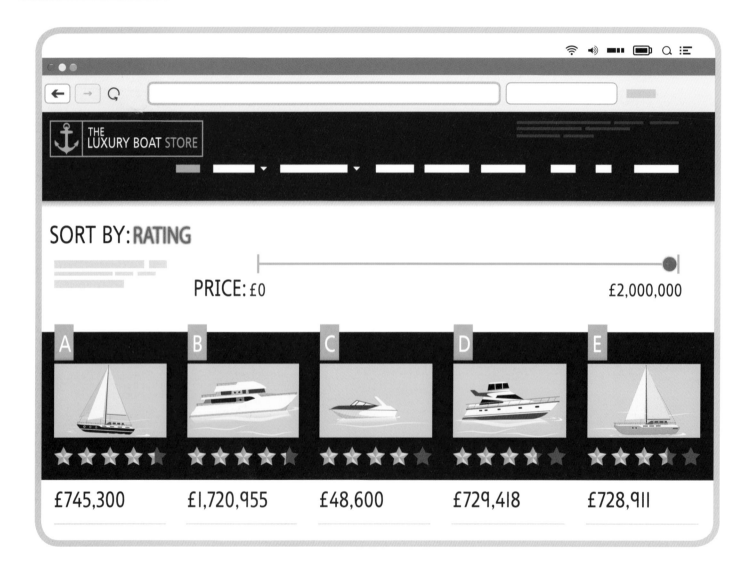

1 **a)** The boats are currently sorted by star rating.

Sort the boats by price, starting with the most expensive.

b) Where would each of the boats appear on the price bar?

Share

a) Compare the millions first.

	M	HTh	TTh	Th	H	T	O
A		7	4	5	3	0	0
B	1	7	2	0	9	5	5
C			4	8	6	0	0
D		7	2	9	4	1	8
E		7	2	8	9	1	1

The most expensive boat is B.

For the other boats, compare the hundred thousands.

	M	HTh	TTh	Th	H	T	O
A		7	4	5	3	0	0
C			4	8	6	0	0
D		7	2	9	4	1	8
E		7	2	8	9	1	1

A, D and E all have 700,000 so look at the next column. Boat A has more ten thousands than D and E.

For boats D and E, now look at the thousands column.

	M	HTh	TTh	Th	H	T	O
D		7	2	9	4	1	8
E		7	2	8	9	1	1

D has more thousands than E.

So the boats in order, from most to least expensive, are B, A, D, E and C.

b) This is where each boat appears on the price bar.

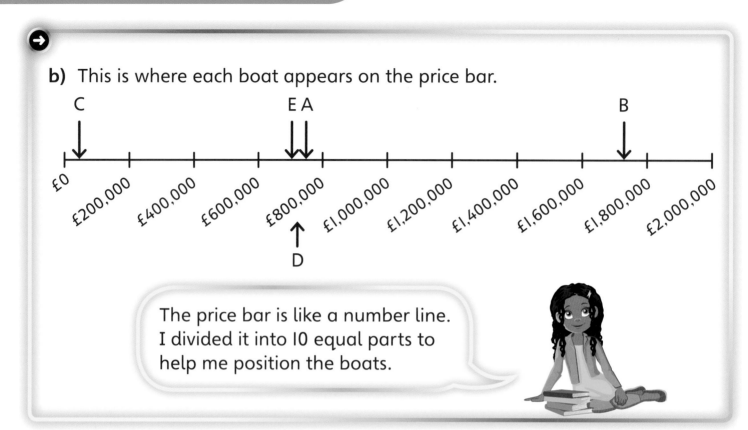

> The price bar is like a number line. I divided it into 10 equal parts to help me position the boats.

Think together

1 Use the signs < and > to compare these boat prices.

a) £429,118 ◯ £518,128

b) £392,271 ◯ £392,098

c) £41,510 ◯ £4,151

d) £7,000,000 ◯ £5,999,999

> I could write the number pairs in a place value grid to help me.

2 Write the prices of these boats in order, starting with the most expensive.

| £320,400 | £302,040 | £32,000 | £302,400 |

26

3 What could the missing digits be to make these statements correct?

a) 7,☐32 > 7,748   7,☐32 > 7,730

b) 12,4☐4 < 12,584   12,4☐4 < 12,484

I think there is more than one correct answer. I will try to find them all.

4 Here are the salaries of four professional football players.

CHALLENGE

Player 1	Player 2	Player 3	Player 4
£3 million	two and a half million pounds	£900,000	£3.6 million

a) Which player earns the most in a year?

b) Which player earns the least in a year?

Salary is the amount a person is paid per year.

I will write each salary in numerals.

I think the player who earns the most is player 3 because their number starts with a 9. I wonder if I am right.

27

Rounding numbers

Discover

1 **a)** Round the population of Zac's town to the nearest 10,000 and 1,000.

b) The number of termites has been rounded to 500,000 to the nearest 100,000.

What are the minimum and maximum numbers of termites there could actually be?

28

Share

a) The population of Zac's town is 76,392. To round to the nearest 10,000, look at the thousands.

TTh	Th	H	T	O
7	6	3	9	2

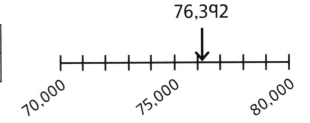

There are 5 or more thousands, so 76,392 rounds up to 80,000.

To round to the nearest 1,000, look at the hundreds.

TTh	Th	H	T	O
7	6	3	9	2

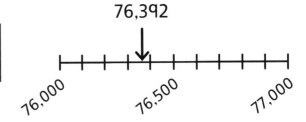

There are fewer than 5 hundreds, so 76,392 rounds down to 76,000.

b) The red part of the line shows all the numbers that would round to 500,000.

400,000   450,000   500,000   550,000   600,000

The minimum number of termites is 450,000.

550,000 rounds up to 600,000. So the maximum number of termites is one fewer than this, 549,999.

> I wonder why the guide has rounded the number of termites.

Think together

  a) Ambika says the population of her town is 10,559.

Round this number to the nearest 10.

TTh	Th	H	T	O
1	0	5	5	9

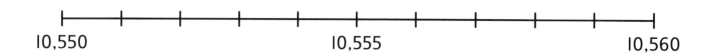

10,550   10,555   10,560

> To round to the nearest 10, I need to decide which digit to look at.

10,559 rounded to the nearest 10 is ☐.

b) One of the longest books ever written has 1,556,028 words.

Round this number to the nearest 100,000.

M	HTh	TTh	Th	H	T	O
1	5	5	6	0	2	8

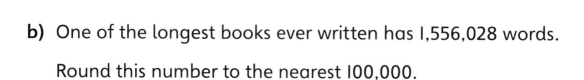

1,500,000   1,550,000   1,600,000

1,556,028 rounded to the nearest 100,000 is ☐.

2 Complete the table for the number below.

179,903

Rounded to the nearest...				
100,000	10,000	1,000	100	10

3

CHALLENGE

2   4   5   7   9

a) Use the digit cards to make a number that rounds to 50,000 to the nearest 10,000.

b) Now use them to make a different number that rounds to 50,000 to the nearest 1,000.

c) Can you use the cards to make a number that rounds to 50,000 to the nearest 100? Explain your answer.

31

→ Practice book 6A p21

Negative numbers

Discover

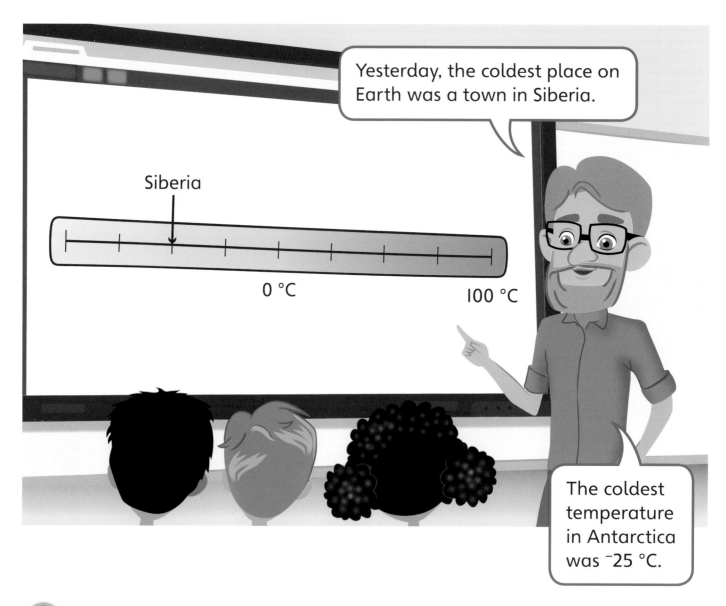

1 a) What was the temperature in the town in Siberia?

b) Where should the temperature in Antarctica be labelled on the thermometer?

Share

a)

To work out what the intervals on the thermometer represent, I used trial and error.

I noticed that there are 4 intervals between 0 and 100, so I divided 100 by 4. This means each interval represents 25 degrees.

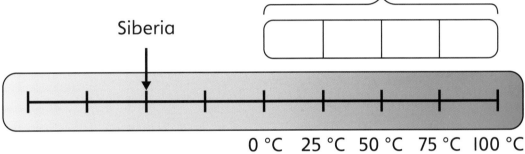

Siberia

0 °C   25 °C   50 °C   75 °C   100 °C

We can write on all the numbers to help us.

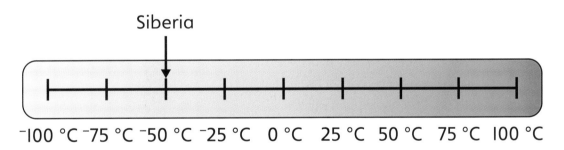

Siberia

⁻100 °C ⁻75 °C ⁻50 °C ⁻25 °C   0 °C   25 °C   50 °C   75 °C   100 °C

I did it a different way. I know that half-way between 0 and 100 is 50. I also know that the arrow is pointing at a number less than 0, so it must point to ⁻50.

The temperature in the town in Siberia was ⁻50 °C.

b) The temperature in Antarctica was ⁻25 °C. Now that we have labelled all the intervals, we can see where this is on the thermometer.

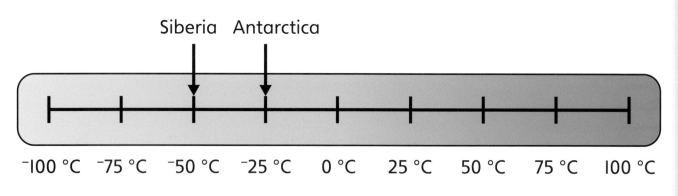

Think together

1 The table shows yesterday's temperature in three cities.

City	Temperature (°C)
Helsinki	⁻5
Paris	2
Moscow	⁻12

a) What was the difference in temperature between Paris and Moscow?

b) The temperature in Helsinki has risen by 8 degrees today.

What is the temperature in Helsinki today?

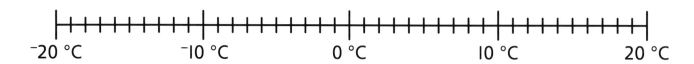

2 **a)** What are the numbers marked A and B?

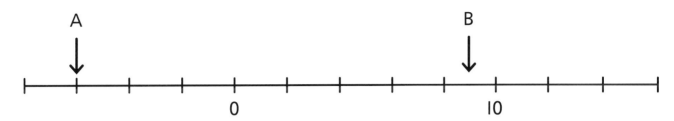

b) Label the number line and mark the numbers ⁻35 and 8.

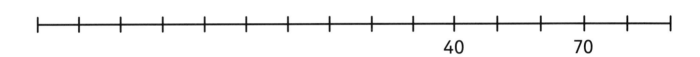

40   70

3 The difference between A and B is 30.

Find the value of C.

CHALLENGE

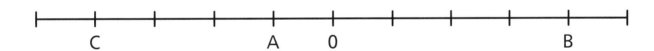

C   A   0   B

First I will work out how many intervals there are between A and B and then I will divide.

35

End of unit check

1 In 531,208, what value does the digit 3 represent?

A 30,000   B 3,000   C 300   D 30

2 What is three million, thirty thousand and three written in numerals?

A 3,300,003   B 3,030,030   C 3,030,003   D 3,000,033

3 What is the missing number in this calculation?

728,305 = 700,000 + 20,000 + ☐ + 300 + 5

A 8   B 80   C 800   D 8,000

4 What is 5,994,061 rounded to the nearest 100,000?

M	HTh	TTh	Th	H	T	O
5	9	9	4	0	6	1

A 5,900,000   B 5,994,100   C 6,000,000   D 6,000,061

5 What number is the arrow pointing to?

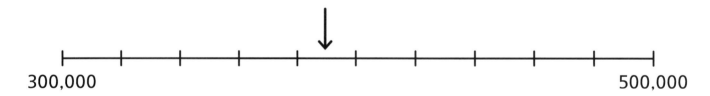

300,000   500,000

A 345,000   B 390,000   C 395,000   D 399,000

6 Which one of the following sets of numbers is in ascending order (goes from smallest to biggest)?

A	500,000	520,000	502,000	500,200
B	500,200	502,000	520,000	500,000
C	500,000	500,200	502,000	520,000
D	520,000	502,000	500,200	500,020

7 Use each digit card once to complete the number sentences.

4　5　7　8　9

A 1 8 ☐ < 1 ☐ 6

B 2 , ☐ 7 6 > 2 , ☐ 9 2

C 3 0 9 5 , 1 4 2 > 3 0 ☐ 7 , 8 3 4

8 a) What are the numbers marked X, Y and Z?

b) What is the difference between Y and Z?

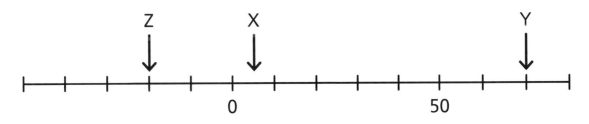

37

→ Practice book 6A p27

Unit 2
Four operations ❶

In this unit we will ...

⚡ Use written methods for addition and subtraction

⚡ Learn to use column multiplication

⚡ Learn different written methods for division

⚡ Learn checking strategies for our calculations

Do you remember what this model is called? We will use it to represent different multiplication calculations. What calculation is being shown here?

	3,000	400	50	6
7	21,000	2,800	350	42

We will need some maths words. Can you identify and explain the ones you already recognise?

column addition　　**column multiplication**

short division　　**long division**

remainder　　**factor**　　**estimate**

We could use this to help us represent division calculations. Can you explain how it has been used here?

$750 \div 15$

750		

250	250	250

50	50	50	50	50	50	50	50	50	50	50	50	50	50	50

Problem solving – using written methods of addition and subtraction ❶

Discover

We have had 2,679 runners this year, but 534 were unable to complete the race.

Mud Mayhem race!

We have 32,145 empty water bottles. 4,302 bottles have not been used. We must have started with 75,165. That seems like a lot.

Water

❶ **a)** How many runners completed the race?

b) Isla thinks they started with 75,165 bottles of water. What calculation can you do to find out if she is right?

Explain the mistake that Isla could have made.

Share

a) We need to do the subtraction 2,679 – 534.

I know different methods to solve additions and subtractions.

I wonder which method suits this particular subtraction.

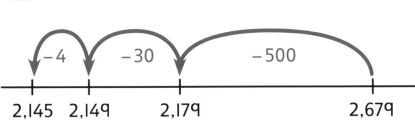

2,145   2,149   2,179   2,679

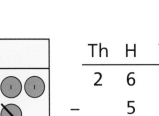

Th	H	T	O

Th	H	T	O
	2	6	7	9
–		5	3	4
	2	1	4	5

2,145 runners completed the race.

b)

TTh	Th	H	T	O
	3	2	1	4	5
+		4	3	0	2
	3	6	4	4	7

Correct calculation

TTh	Th	H	T	O
	3	2	1	4	5
+	4	3	0	2	
	7	5	1	6	5

Isla's calculation

Isla is not right. The correct answer is 32,145 + 4,302 = 36,447

Isla has tried to use column addition, but she has not lined up the digits correctly.

Think together

① The runners at the Mud Mayhem race raised £40,265 for charity. The runners at a sponsored marathon raised £3,522 more than that.

How much money did the marathon runners raise? Use two methods to work it out.

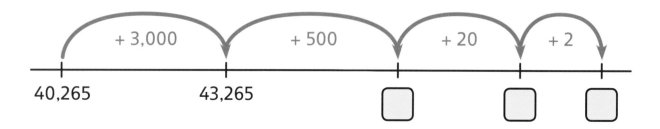

TTh	Th	H	T	O
10,000 10,000 10,000 10,000		100 100	10 10 10 10 10 / 10	1 1 1 1 1 1
	1,000 1,000 1,000	100 100 100 100 100	10 10	1 1

```
  TTh Th  H  T  O
    4  0  2  6  5
+      3  5  2  2
  _____
  _____
```

② 1,618 runners started a marathon, but 306 of them did not finish.

a) How many runners finished the marathon?

b) How many more runners started the Mud Mayhem race than started the marathon?

c) What is the total number of runners who finished the two races?

 3 **a)** An organiser is trying to calculate how many more spectators there were at a Mud Mayhem race than at a marathon.

There is mud on his calculation. Work out the missing information.

TTh	Th	H	T	O
4	5	7	8	✳
✳ 4	0	✳	5	2
✳	✳	7	✳	1

b) Here is a calculation for the total number of spectators at three different races.

	HTh	TTh	Th	H	T	O
	3	1	2	0	5	7
	4	2	2	1	2	1
+			4	8	0	1
	7	3	8	9	7	9

Cover up some of the digits in this calculation but leave enough information so that someone else can work out what the missing digits are.

> I am going to see how many digits I can cover up before it is impossible for someone to work out what the calculation is.

43

Problem solving – using written methods of addition and subtraction ❷

Discover

Elizabeth I became Queen in 1558. She was monarch until she died, 45 years later.

1 **a)** In what year did Queen Elizabeth I die?

b) Queen Elizabeth II's reign began in 1952. How many years were there between the beginning of Elizabeth I's reign and the beginning of Elizabeth II's reign?

Share

a) To answer this, use the addition 1,558 + 45.

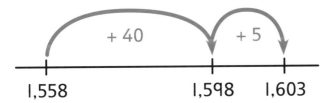

1,558   1,598   1,603

Th	H	T	O

Th	H	T	O
1	5	5	8
+		4	5
1	6	0	3
		1	1

> I need to exchange 10 ones, because 8 ones + 5 ones = 13 ones.

> Look out! The tens also need an exchange now. There are 5 tens + 4 tens + 1 more ten.

Queen Elizabeth I died in the year 1603.

b) Find the difference between 1,558 and 1,952 to answer this question.

Th	H	T	O
1	⁸9̶	¹⁴5̶	¹2
– 1	5	5	8
	3	9	4

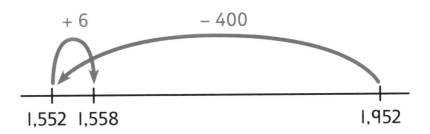

+ 6   – 400

1,552 1,558   1,952

There were 394 years between the beginning of Elizabeth I's reign and the beginning of Elizabeth II's reign.

Think together

1 Ethelred the Unready was monarch from 978 to 1013. How many years did he reign for?

Th	H	T	O
(1,000)		(10)	(1)(1)(1)

```
Th  H  T  O
    1  0  1  3
  -    9  7  8
  _____
```

Ethelred the Unready reigned for ⬚ years.

I will try two methods to check my answer is correct.

2 This timeline shows the reigns of different royal houses of England.

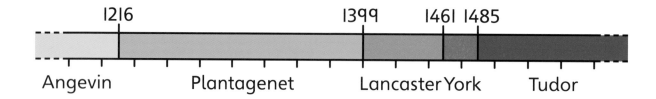

a) How long was the rule of the House of Lancaster?

The rule of the House of Lancaster was ⬚ years long.

b) The Tudor reign lasted 118 years. When did it end?

The Tudor reign ended in ⬚ .

3 **a)** Write a 4-digit number using four different digits. Then reverse the digits to make a second 4-digit number.

Find the difference between your two numbers.

> I wrote 2,609. The reverse is 9,062.
>
> So, I need to work out 9,062 − 2,609.
>
> | Th | H | T | O |
> |----|---|---|---|
> | 9 | 0 | 6 | 2 |
> | − 2 | 6 | 0 | 9 |

Did your subtraction require any exchanges?

Try a few different examples. Do you always need to exchange across two columns?

Can you explain this?

b) Now do the same with two 7-digit numbers.

Try to find a number where you will only need one exchange.

Then try to find a number where you will need two exchanges.

> I am going to try to go all the way up to seven exchanges.
> I wonder whether it is possible.

47

Multiplying numbers up to 4 digits by a 1-digit number

Discover

A trip from London to Beijing costs £3,225 per person.

That is £128,820 for four people. It is too expensive.

I think it is only £12,905 for four people.

1 **a)** Without calculating, how can you tell which total is more likely to be correct, £128,820 or £12,905?

b) How much will the trip actually cost for four people?

Share

a)

I will estimate by rounding 3,225 to 3,000. That means the trip for four people would be about £12,000, so it cannot be £128,820.

I know that multiplying the ones digit 5 by 4 means the ones digit of the answer must be 0, so I do not think £12,905 is correct.

Using rounding to estimate shows that £12,905 is more likely to be correct. However, we know it is not correct because the answer must end in 0.

b)

Method 1

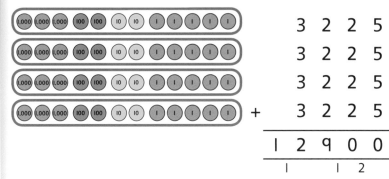

$$
\begin{array}{ccccc}
 & 3 & 2 & 2 & 5 \\
 & 3 & 2 & 2 & 5 \\
 & 3 & 2 & 2 & 5 \\
+ & 3 & 2 & 2 & 5 \\
\hline
1 & 2 & 9 & 0 & 0 \\
\hline
 & 1 & & 1 & 2
\end{array}
$$

Method 3

	3,000	200	20	5
4	12,000	800	80	20

$12,000 + 800 + 80 + 20 = 12,900$

Method 2

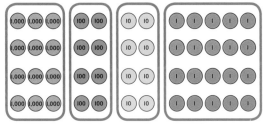

$4 \times 3,000 \quad 4 \times 200 \quad 4 \times 20 \quad 4 \times 5$

$12,000 + 800 + 80 + 20 = 12,900$

Method 4

$$
\begin{array}{ccccc}
 & 3 & 2 & 2 & 5 \\
\times & & & & 4 \\
\hline
1 & 2 & 9 & 0 & 0 \\
\hline
 & & 1 & & 2
\end{array}
$$

$3,225 \times 4 = 12,900$. The trip will cost £12,900 for four people.

Think together

1 The holiday costs £2,345 per person with a different travel company.

What is the total cost for 4 people?

Th	H	T	O
1,000 1,000 1,000 1,000 1,000 1,000 1,000 1,000	100 100 100 100 100 100 100 100 100 100 100 100	10 10 10 10 10 10 10 10 10 10 10 10 10 10 10 10	1 1 1 1 1 1 1 1 1 1 1 1 1 1 1 1 1 1 1 1 1 1 1 1

```
Th  H  T  O
    2  3  4  5
    2  3  4  5
    2  3  4  5
+   2  3  4  5
_____
```

2,000	300	40	5
4 | | | | |

```
    2  3  4  5
×             4
_____
_____
```

Use all the different methods. Which one do you prefer?

The total cost for 4 people is £ ⬚ .

2 a) Another trip costs £2,865 per person. How much would the cost be for five people?

b) How much would it cost for six people?

I wonder if I could work out the cost for 6 people by adding to the answer for 5 people.

I will use column multiplication. It is more efficient.

3 **a)** Use each card once to complete the multiplication.

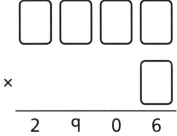

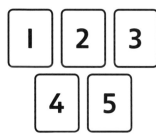

I think there is more than one possible answer.

b) Rearrange the cards and use each card once to make a new calculation with a different answer.

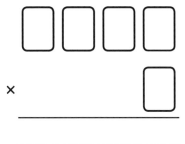

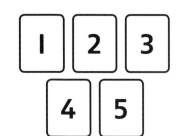

c) Can you make a calculation with a 5-digit answer? Can you make a calculation with a 6-digit answer?

I am going to find what is the biggest answer I can make.

51

Multiplying numbers up to 4 digits by a 2-digit number

Discover

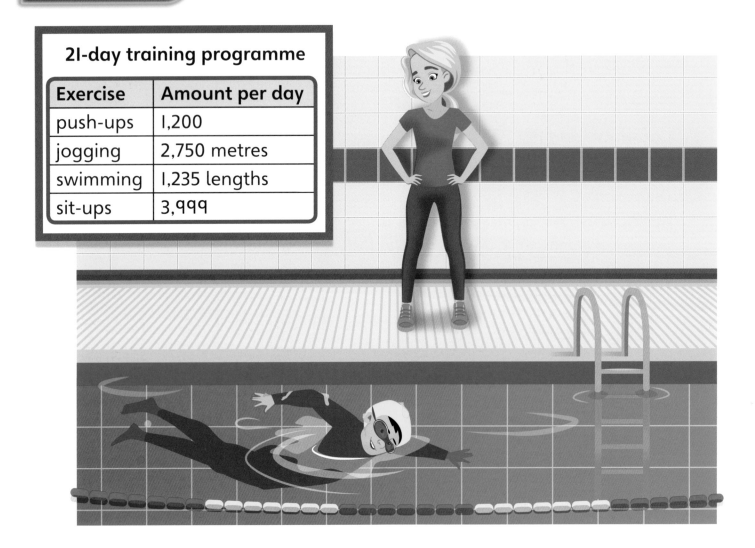

21-day training programme	
Exercise	**Amount per day**
push-ups	1,200
jogging	2,750 metres
swimming	1,235 lengths
sit-ups	3,999

1 **a)** Use column multiplication to find how many lengths the athletes in the swimming team swim altogether in 21 days.

b) The coach says, 'I can work it out more quickly if I first work out how many lengths the athletes swim in one week.'

Use the coach's method. Does it give the same answer?

Share

a) Find 21 lots of 1,235.

Method I

	1,000	200	30	5
20	20,000	4,000	600	100
1	1,000	200	30	5

> I used the grid method. Sometimes people call it the area method.

Method 2

	1,235
20	1,235 × 20
1	1,235 × 1

> I used long multiplication. It was quicker than the grid method.

```
      1 2 3 5
  ×       2 1
  ─────────────
            5    1 × 5
          3 0    1 × 30
        2 0 0    1 × 200
      1 0 0 0    1 × 1,000
          1 0 0  20 × 5
          6 0 0  20 × 30
        4 0 0 0  20 × 200
      2 0 0 0 0  20 × 1,000
  ─────────────
      2 5 9 3 5  21 × 1,235
  ─────────────
```

```
      1 2 3 5
  ×       2 1
  ─────────────
      1 2 3 5    1 × 1,235
    2 4 7 0 0    20 × 1,235
  ─────────────
    2 5 9 3 5    21 × 1,235
  ─────────────
```

21 × 1,235 = 25,935. The athletes swim 25,935 lengths in 21 days.

b) 21 × 1,235 = 3 × 7 × 1,235

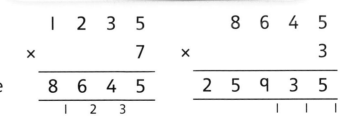

		1,235
21 ⎰	7	1,235 × 7 = 8,645
	7	1,235 × 7 = 8,645
	7	1,235 × 7 = 8,645

> There are seven days in one week. 3 × 7 = 21, so I can partition 21 into 3 lots of 7.

This method gives the same answer.

```
    1 2 3 5
  ×       7
  ─────────
    8 6 4 5
    1 2 3
```

```
    8 6 4 5
  ×       3
  ─────────
  2 5 9 3 5
    1 1 1
```

53

Think together

1 The coach changes the training programme so the athletes will now train for 24 days. How many lengths will the athletes swim in total now?

24-day training programme

Exercise	Amount per day
push-ups	1,200
jogging	2,750 metres
swimming	1,235 lengths
sit-ups	3,999

	1,000	200	30	5
20				
4				

```
      1  2  3  5
  ×         2  4
  _____
```

4 × 5
4 × 30
4 × 200
4 × 1,000
20 × 5
20 × 30
20 × 200
20 × 1,000

_____

The athletes will swim ☐ lengths in total now.

2 How many sit-ups will the athletes do in 35 days?

```
      3  9  9  9
  ×         3  5
  _____

  _____
  _____
```

5 × 3,999
30 × 3,999

> I will work out 4,000 × 35 to make it easier to find the number of sit-ups.

3 Isla is calculating the area of this rectangle.

5,200 cm

25 cm

CHALLENGE

She uses five different methods to find the solution.

Try out each of Isla's methods. Do they all produce the same answer?

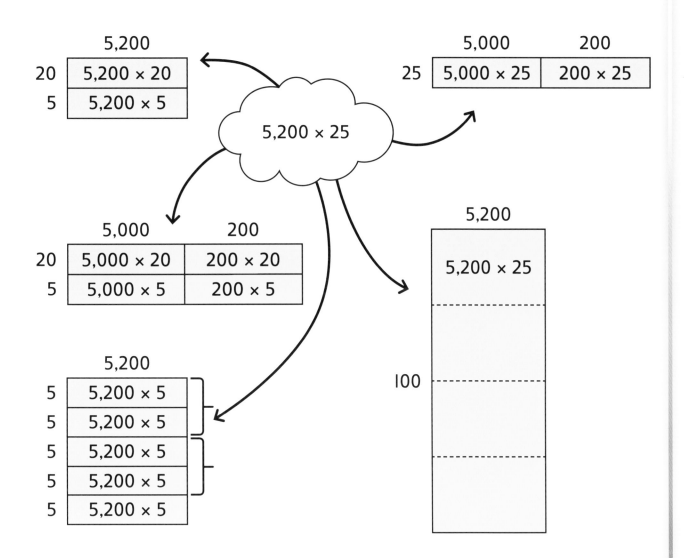

Work out the answer using long multiplication.

Which of all the methods do you prefer?

→ Practice book 6A p38

Dividing numbers up to 4 digits by a 2-digit number ❶

Discover

a) Each astronaut has 132 bottles of water for their stay in the space station. How many days will this last for one astronaut?

b) The astronauts eat the same amount of fruit puree each week. How many tubes of fruit puree will they eat each week?

Share

a) This model can help to work out how many 6s are in 132.

```
      ?
6 |  132  |

6 × ? = 132
```

```
      10          10        1  1
6 |   60   |      60      | 6 | 6 |
```

```
         20              2
6 |      120      |     12    |
```

132 = 120 + 12

132 ÷ 6 = 20 + 2 = 22

We can also use the method of short division.

H	T	O
100	10 10 10	1 1

How many groups of 6 are in 100?

```
      0
6 | 1 ¹3  2
```

H	T	O
100 →	10 10 10 10 10 10 10 10 10 10 10 10 10	1 1

How many groups of 6 are in 13 tens?

```
      0  2
6 | 1 ¹3 ¹2
```

H	T	O
	10 10 10 10 10 10 10 10 10 10 10 10 10 →	1 1 1 1 1 1 1 1 1 1 1 1

How many groups of 6 are in 12 ones?

```
      0  2  2
6 | 1 ¹3 ¹2
```

132 ÷ 6 = 22

132 bottles of water will last for **22** days for one astronaut.

b)

20	1
280	14

14

$$14 \overline{\smash{\big)}\, 2\ {}^2 9\ {}^1 4} \quad \begin{matrix} 0\ 2\ 1 \end{matrix}$$

I wonder why there is a 2 in the tens.

I know that 14 × 20 = 280, so I can tell that there will be 2 tens in the answer.

$294 \div 14 = 21$

The astronauts will eat 21 tubes of fruit puree in one week.

Think together

1   In total, there are 3,350 kg of supplies on the space station. If the astronauts use 5 kg of supplies per day, how many days will the supplies last for?

☐	☐	☐

3,000	300	50

5

$$5 \overline{\smash{\big)}\, 3\ 3\ 5\ 0}$$

The supplies will last for ☐ days.

2   A rocket can carry 560 kg.

If each satellite weighs 40 kg, how many satellites can a rocket carry?

$$40 \overline{\smash{\big)}\, 5\ 6\ 0}$$

A rocket can carry ☐ satellites.

3 **a)** Solve these divisions.

$5,050 \div 25 = \boxed{}$

$1,770 \div 15 = \boxed{}$

$\boxed{} = 9,840 \div 24$

I will need to find $0 \div 24$ for the last division. I wonder if that is possible.

b) These is no remainder in either of these divisions. Work out the missing digits.

$$11 \overline{\smash)\begin{array}{ccccc} 0 & 4 & \text{✹} & 4 \\ 4 & 6 & \text{✹} & 4 \end{array}}$$

I will start by working out how many groups of 11 are in 46.

$$12 \overline{\smash)\begin{array}{cccc} & 2 & 0 & \text{✹} \\ \text{✹} & 4 & 7 & \text{✹} \end{array}}$$

→ **Practice book 6A p41**

Dividing numbers up to 4 digits by a 2-digit number ②

Discover

750 people rode in the log flume boat today. It was full every time.

1 **a)** How many times did the log flume boat run today?

   b) The log flume boat was running for 5 hours. How many people rode in the boat per hour?

Share

a)

There are 15 seats on the log flume boat. I will work out 750 ÷ 15.

I can see a way to make this easier.

I know that 15 is 3 × 5 so I will divide by using factors.

750

750

250	250	250

$750 ÷ 3 = 250$

50	50	50	50	50	50	50	50	50	50	50	50	50	50	50

$250 ÷ 5 = 50$

$750 ÷ 15 = 750 ÷ 3 ÷ 5$

The log flume boat ran 50 times today.

b) Use the fact $3 × 5 × 50 = 750$.

50	50	50	50	50
50	50	50	50	50
50	50	50	50	50

⟶

50				
50				
50				

$3 × 50 = 150$

$5 × 150 = 750$

So

$750 ÷ 5 = 150$

150 people rode in the log flume boat per hour.

I could have used short division to divide 750 by 5.

Think together

1 A new roller coaster opens at the park. 1,260 people ride on it in the first 14 days. How many people is that per day?

> I know 14 is 2 × 7. I will divide by 2, and then divide by 7.

1,260

1,260 ÷ 2 = ▢

▢ ÷ 7 = ▢

▢ people ride on the new roller coaster per day.

2 Tickets for the park cost £18 per person. On one day the park made £5,490. How many tickets were sold?

Choose which method solves the division correctly, then solve it.

5,490 ⟶ ┆ ÷ 6 ┆ ⟶ ┆ ÷ 3 ┆ ⟶

5,490 ⟶ ┆ ÷ 10 ┆ ⟶ ┆ ÷ 8 ┆ ⟶

5,490 ÷ ▢ ÷ ▢ = ▢

▢ tickets were sold on that day.

62

3 **a)** Max is trying to solve 2,100 ÷ 12.

CHALLENGE

I will use the facts that 12 is 2 × 6, 6 × 2, 3 × 4 and 4 × 3.

I can see that 12 is also 3 × 2 × 2.

2,100 ⟶ ÷ 2 ⟶ ÷ 6 ⟶

2,100 ⟶ ÷ 6 ⟶ ÷ 2 ⟶

2,100 ⟶ ÷ 3 ⟶ ÷ 4 ⟶

2,100 ⟶ ÷ 4 ⟶ ÷ 3 ⟶

2,100 ⟶ ÷ 3 ⟶ ÷ 2 ⟶ ÷ 2 ⟶

Max tries each of these calculations.

Do they all give the correct answer?

Which method makes it easiest to solve?

b) Reena is trying to solve 1,800 ÷ 24. Which factors could she choose?

1,800 ⟶ ÷ ? ⟶ ÷ ?

1,800 ⟶ ÷ ? ⟶ ÷ ? ⟶ ÷ ?

1,800 ⟶ ÷ ? ⟶ ÷ ? ⟶ ÷ ? ⟶ ÷ ?

→ Practice book 6A p44

Dividing numbers up to 4 digits by a 2-digit number ❸

Discover

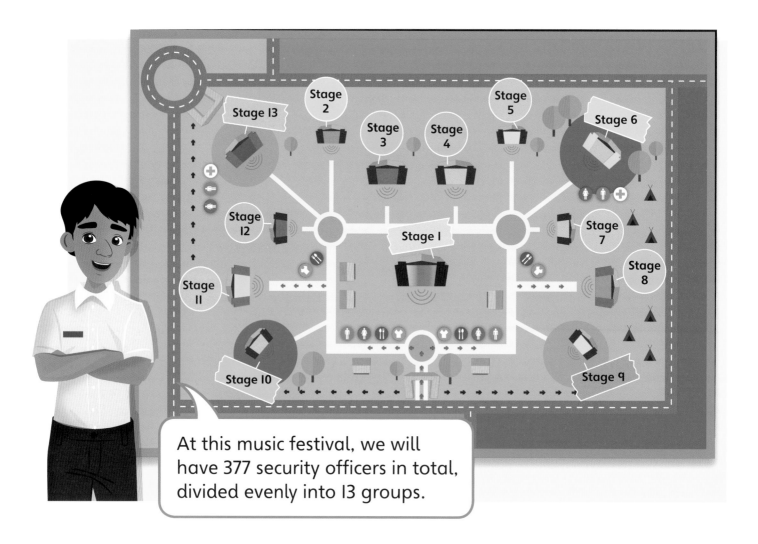

At this music festival, we will have 377 security officers in total, divided evenly into 13 groups.

1 **a)** How many security officers will there be in each group?

b) What multiplication can you do to check your answer is correct?

Share

I listed the first 10 multiples of 13 to help me with the division.

a) There are 377 security officers in total. Divide these equally into 13 groups.

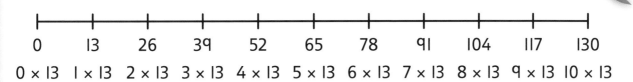

0	13	26	39	52	65	78	91	104	117	130
0 × 13	1 × 13	2 × 13	3 × 13	4 × 13	5 × 13	6 × 13	7 × 13	8 × 13	9 × 13	10 × 13

?

13	377

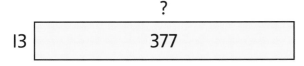

	10	?
13	130	247

```
13 │ 3  7  7
   − 1  3  0    10
     2  4  7
```

I first subtracted 130, which is 10 groups of 13.

	10	10	?
13	130	130	117

```
13 │ 3  7  7
   − 1  3  0    10
     2  4  7
   − 1  3  0    10
     1  1  7
```

I then subtracted another 10 groups of 13.

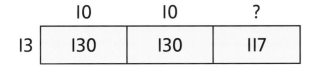

29

	10	10	9
13	130	130	117

So 377 ÷ 13 = 29

There will be 29 security officers in each group.

```
13 │ 3  7  7
   − 1  3  0    10
     2  4  7
   − 1  3  0    10
     1  1  7
   − 1  1  7     9
     0          29
```

Finally I subtracted 9 groups of 13 as this was equal to 117. I could have subtracted 5, and then 4 groups of 9.

b) You can do the multiplication 29 × 13 = 377 to check your answer is correct.

Think together

1 The organisers of the festival want to release 437 balloons in 23 equal groups. How many balloons will there be in each group?

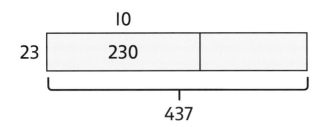

23 | 4 3 7
    − 2 3 0   10

Remember you can write out your multiples of 23 to help you before you begin.

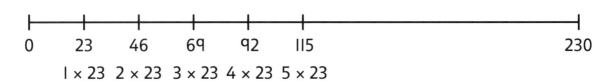

1 × 23 2 × 23 3 × 23 4 × 23 5 × 23

There will be ☐ balloons in each group.

2 A stall is selling flower decorations. They have shared 682 roses between 31 flower decorations. How many roses are there in each decoration?

There are ☐ roses in each decoration.

3 Reena and Emma are discussing which division methods to use.

CHALLENGE

> To work out 588 ÷ 28, I will divide by 4, then divide by 7.

Reena

> I want to work out 799 ÷ 17. Should I use Reena's method, or should I use a different method?

Emma

Which method would you tell Emma to use? Why?

Solve both divisions.

> I do not think I can use Reena's method for Emma's calculation. I wonder why not.

> If I know what 4 groups of 17 are, I can work out 40 groups of 17 too. It might be quicker to subtract this.

67

→ Practice book 6A p47

Dividing numbers up to 4 digits by a 2-digit number ④

Discover

Our rescue centre got a donation of 2,478 tins of cat food.

1 **a)** The cat rescue centre uses 21 tins of food each day. How many days will the food last for?

b) After a while, there are 798 tins of food left. Is this enough to last 7 weeks?

68

Share

I will use repeated subtraction.

a) There are 2,478 tins of food. 21 tins are used each day.

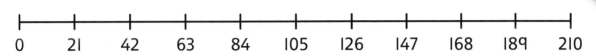

| 0 | 21 | 42 | 63 | 84 | 105 | 126 | 147 | 168 | 189 | 210 |

0 × 21   1 × 21   2 × 21   3 × 21   4 × 21   5 × 21   6 × 21   7 × 21   8 × 21   9 × 21   10 × 21

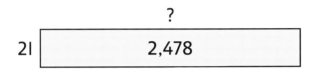

?

21 | 2,478 |

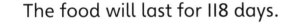

	100	10	8
21	2,100	210	168

2,478 ÷ 21 = 118

```
21 | 2  4  7  8
  -  2  1  0  0    100
        3  7  8
  -     2  1  0     10
        1  6  8
  -     1  6  8      8
              0    118
```

The food will last for 118 days.

b) Divide 798 by 21 to work out the number of days.

```
          3
  21 | 7  9  8
   -  6  3  0
      1  6  8
```

Subtract the biggest number of tens of multiples of 21 from 798 first.

If 3 × 21 = 63, 30 × 21 = 630.

Put the 3 tens above the line.

```
          3  8
  21 | 7  9  8
   -  6  3  0
      1  6  8
   -  1  6  8
            0
```

168 is left.

8 × 21 = 168 so subtract this now.

Put the 8 ones above the line.

798 ÷ 21 = 38

The food will last for 38 days. This is not enough for 7 weeks (49 days).

I will use a method called **long division**.

Think together

1 The rescue centre buys 812 bags of cat food. If they use 29 bags each day, how many days will this last for?

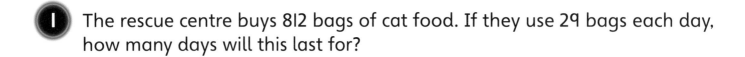

0   29   58   87   116   145   174   203   232   261   290

29 [   ]   29 | 8 1 2

The bags will last for ☐ days.

2 The rescue centre buys 4,439 bags of cat litter to last for 23 months. How many bags of cat litter does the centre use each month?

```
            100
23 |    2,300    |      |
```

```
              1
   23 | 4  4  3  9
      − 2  3  0  0
        _____
        2  1  3  9
```

The centre uses ☐ bags of cat litter each month.

I wonder if long division is always a good method to use.

70

3 Choose a division method to solve each of these calculations.

$1,311 \div 23 = \boxed{}$

$1,890 \div 45 = \boxed{}$

$\boxed{} = 2,346 \div 23$

$7,379 \div 47 = \boxed{}$

$4,000 \div 80 = \boxed{}$

$\boxed{} = 2,525 \div 25$

I am going to use long division for each one.

I do not think that is always the most efficient method. I think you can solve some of these much more quickly.

71

Dividing numbers up to 4 digits by a 2-digit number ⑤

Discover

I **a)** A scientist finds that cicadas have emerged this year. How many times will they emerge again over the next 100 years?

b) How many times will they emerge over the next 200 years?

Share

I will start with a fact I know, 3 × 17 = 51.

I think there will be a remainder, because 100 is not a multiple of 17.

a) **Method 1**

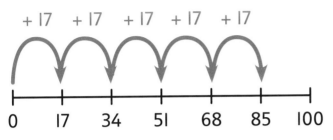

+ 17   + 17   + 17   + 17   + 17

0   17   34   51   68   85   100

3	2	
51	34	15

17

100 = 51 + 34 + 15

100 ÷ 17 = 3 + 2 remainder 15

= 5 remainder 15

Method 2

```
17 | 1 0 0
   -   5 1      3
       4 9
   -   3 4      2
     | 1 5 |
              5
```

100 ÷ 17 = 5 remainder 15

Method 3

```
            5 r 15
17 | 1 0 0
   -   8 5
       1 5
```

The cicadas will emerge again 5 times over the next 100 years. There will then be 15 years left until 100 years have passed.

b)

I thought it would be 10 times in 200 years, but 200 divided by 17 gives a remainder of 30, which is bigger than 17.

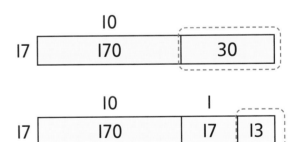

10	30
170	30

17

10	1	
170	17	13

17

200 ÷ 17 = 11 remainder 13

The cicadas will emerge 11 times over the next 200 years. There will then be 13 years left until 200 years have passed.

Think together

1 There is a butterfly in North America that emerges every 13 years. How many times will the butterfly appear in 100 years?

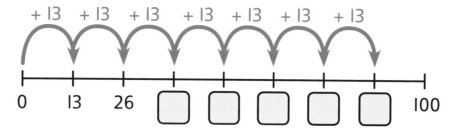

+ 13   + 13   + 13   + 13   + 13   + 13   + 13

0   13   26   ☐   ☐   ☐   ☐   ☐   100

remainder ☐

13 | 1 0 0
   –
   _____

$100 \div 13 = $ ☐ remainder ☐

The butterfly will appear ☐ times in 100 years.

There will then be ☐ years left until 100 years have passed.

2 There is a lighthouse jellyfish that has lived to 306 years old. A hurricane occurs every 19 years in the ocean where it lives. How many hurricanes has this jellyfish experienced?

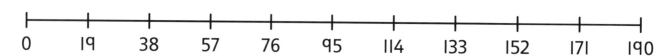

0   19   38   57   76   95   114   133   152   171   190

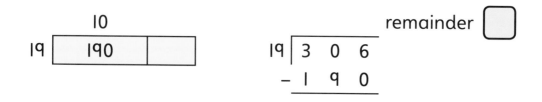

10

19 | 190 |

19 | 3 0 6
   – 1 9 0

remainder ☐

The jellyfish has experienced ☐ hurricanes.

3 **a)** A snake sheds its skin every 68 days. If the snake sheds its skin today, will it also shed its skin in exactly one year's time? If not, how many days later will it shed its skin?

CHALLENGE

I think there are 365 days in one year. I will divide 365 by 68.

I wonder how the answer will change if it is a leap year.

b) Discuss what the remainder tells you in each of these problems.

- A carpenter takes 25 days to make one chair. How many chairs can she make in a year?

- A builder needs 365 planks to build a roof. The planks come in packs of 25. How many packs should he buy?

- A bricklayer lays 365 bricks in 10 hours. How many bricks does he lay per hour?

75

→ **Practice book 6A p53**

Dividing numbers up to 4 digits by a 2-digit number ❻

Discover

Vintage car race, 1,235 km

FA19 SST

VR03 OOM

SP10 EED

Stage 1 of 25

1 **a)** The race is split into 25 equal stages. How long is each stage?

b) How would you deal with a remainder to get an accurate answer in this situation?

Share

a) The race is 1,235 kilometres long. It is split into 25 equal stages.

Divide 1,235 by 25.

	40	9	
25	1,000	225	10

```
        4  9  r 10
   _____
29 | 1  2  3  5
  − 1  0  0  0
   _____
      2  3  5
  −   2  2  5
   _____
         1  0
```

First, I subtracted 40 lots of 25 and then subtracted 9 lots of 25. There was a remainder of 10.

1,235 ÷ 25 = 49 remainder 10.

Each stage is 49 km long with 10 km remaining.

b) To get a more accurate answer, divide the remainder between all 25 stages, so that it is also divided by 25.

This can then be written as a fraction $\frac{10}{25}$

$\frac{10}{25}$ simplifies to $\frac{2}{5}$

Each stage is 49 km plus $\frac{2}{5}$ of a km.

I thought the remainder could be an extra stage at the end, but then the stages would not be equal.

77

Think together

1 The following year, the race is split into 40 equal stages.

Kate, Alex and Luis are working out how long each stage will be now.

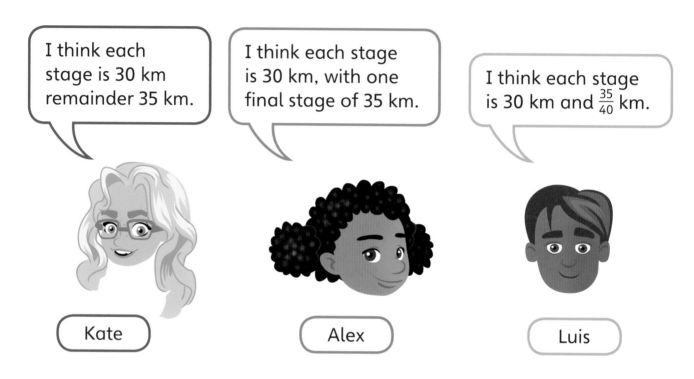

I think each stage is 30 km remainder 35 km.

I think each stage is 30 km, with one final stage of 35 km.

I think each stage is 30 km and $\frac{35}{40}$ km.

Kate

Alex

Luis

Who do you agree with? Why?

2 50 cars take part in the race. The cars use 3,580 litres of fuel altogether. How much fuel does each car use?

Each car uses ☐ and $\frac{\square}{\square}$ litres of fuel.

I wonder how I should deal with the remainder.

3 Ebo did this calculation to work out how to split the 3,580 litres of fuel between the 50 cars.

What does Ebo need to do next to find the correct remainder?

3,580 = 358 tens

50 = 5 tens

3,580 ÷ 50 = 358 ÷ 5

```
        7  1
    ┌──────────
  5 │ 3  5  8
    − 3  5  0
    ──────────
             8
    −        5
    ──────────
             3
```

358 ÷ 50 = 71 remainder 3

Ebo needs to _____

So, 3,580 ÷ 50 = 71 remainder ☐

I think Ebo's calculation, 358 divided by 5, shows that the remainder is 3.

But the real calculation is actually 3,580 divided by 50.

→ **Practice book 6A p56**

End of unit check

1 Which calculation matches this number line?

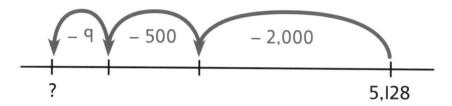

A

Th	H	T	O
⁴5̶	¹⁰1̶	¹¹2̶	¹8
−		2	5	9
4	8	6	9

B

Th	H	T	O
⁴5̶	¹1	¹2̶	¹8
− 2	5	0	9
2	6	1	9

C

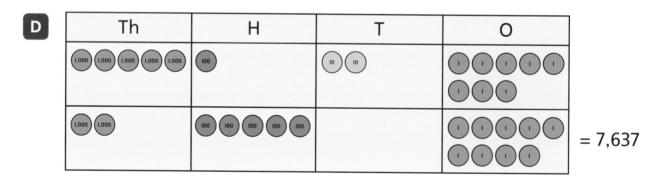

Th	H	T	O

D

Th	H	T	O

= 7,637

2 Which of these calculations is not correct?

A 3,065 × 25 = 76,625

C 3,650 × 25 = 91,250

B 3,605 × 25 = 90,125

D 3,506 × 25 = 87,655

3 Which of these divisions has an error?

A
```
15 │ 7   5   4   5
  -  6   0   0   0    400
     1   5   4   5
  -  1   5   0   0    100
             4   5
  -          4   5      3
             0        503
```

C $4,575 \div 15$

$$4,575 \div 3 = 1,525$$

$$1,525 \div 5 = 305$$

B
```
          1   8   3
25 │ 4   5   7   5
  -  2   5   0   0
     2   0   7   5
  -  2   0   0   0
             7   5
```

D $5,475 \div 15$

$$5,475 \div 5 = 1,803$$

$$1,803 \div 3 = 601$$

4 An aquarium has 2,010 g of fish food. It uses 20 g of food per day. How many whole days will the fish food last for?

A 10 days   **B** 101 days   **C** 100 days   **D** 201 days

5 $275 \times 21 = \boxed{} \times 35$

81

→ Practice book 6A p59

Unit 3
Four operations ②

In this unit we will …
- ⚡ Find common factors and multiples
- ⚡ Learn about prime, square and cube numbers
- ⚡ Learn about the order of operations
- ⚡ Solve mental calculations

Do you remember what this model is called? We will use it to represent different calculations. Can you tell what calculation is being represented here?

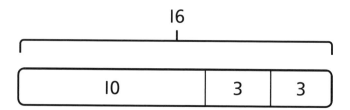

16

| 10 | 3 | 3 |

We will need some maths words. Can you identify and explain the ones you recognise?

factor   common factor   common multiple

prime   composite   squared (x²)

cubed (x³)   order of operations

brackets   inverse operation

We will need to remember multiplication facts. We could use arrays of counters to help us!

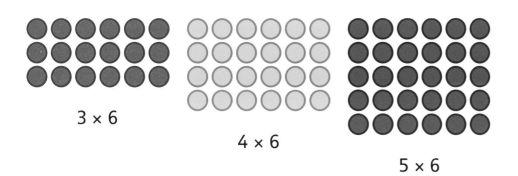

3 × 6

4 × 6

5 × 6

Common factors

Discover

We should divide into groups. We are 24 adults and 30 children.

Let's have 4 groups.

Make sure there are the same number of adults and children in each group.

Treasure Hunt
Adventure Land

I **a)** Can the adults and children split equally into 4 groups?

b) What are the equal groups the adults and children could split into?

Share

a) The adults can divide equally into 4 groups, because 4 is a **factor** of 24.

The children cannot divide equally into 4 groups, because 4 is **not** a factor of 30.

The adults and children cannot split equally into 4 groups.

A factor is a number that divides a number exactly.

4 is a factor of 24, because $24 \div 4 = 6$ with no remainder.

Adults

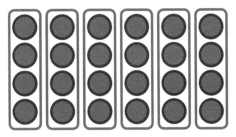

$24 \div 4 = 6$

Children

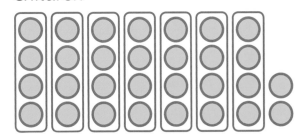

$30 \div 4 = 7$ remainder 2

b) Find the factors of both 24 and 30.

$1 \times 24 = 24$
$2 \times 12 = 24$
$3 \times 8 = 24$
$4 \times 6 = 24$

$1 \times 30 = 30$
$2 \times 15 = 30$
$3 \times 10 = 30$
$5 \times 6 = 30$

I can use multiplication facts to find the factors of a number. Then I will find the factors that are in both lists.

Factors of 24 are 1, 2, 3, 4, 6, 8, 12 and 24.

Factors of 30 are 1, 2, 3, 5, 6, 10, 15 and 30.

1, 2, 3 and 6 are called common factors of 24 and 30. They are in **both** lists.

The adults and children could split into 1, 2, 3 or 6 equal groups.

Think together

1. Share this team of adults and children into equal groups.

Begin by writing multiplication sentences.

> **Team**
>
> 12 adults
> 15 children

1 × 12 = 12

◻ × ◻ = 12

◻ × ◻ = 12

1 × ◻ = 15

◻ × ◻ = 15

Factors of 12 are

_____ .

Factors of 15 are

_____ .

The common factors of 12 and 15 are ◻ and ◻ .

The adults and children could split into ◻ group or ◻ groups.

2. Write the numbers 1–10 in a sorting diagram like this.

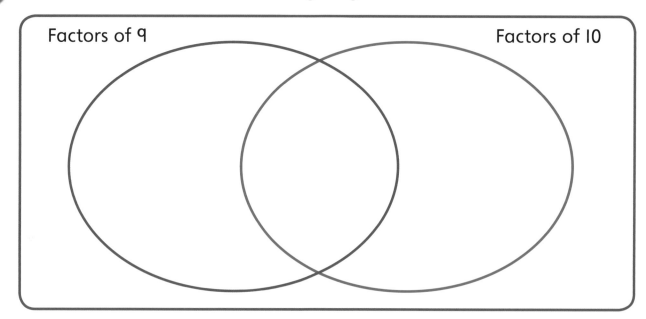

Factors of 9   Factors of 10

Are there any common factors of 9 and 10?

3 Bella wants to find the common factors of the three numbers 10, 15 and 20.

She uses this table to help.

Factors of 10	Factors of 15	Factors of 20

I wonder how Bella will know when she has checked all the numbers she needs to.

I know 2 will not be a factor of 15 because 15 is an odd number. I think that will help.

a) Which numbers will appear in all three lists?

b) Which numbers will appear in just two lists?

c) Are there any numbers that will appear in just one list?

Common multiples

Discover

I **a)** On which days will Lexi need to change the bedding and give carrots?

b) On which days will Lexi need to do all three jobs?

Share

a) Flopsy gets a carrot on days that are a multiple of 3.

1	2	③	4	5	⑥	7	8	⑨	10
11	⑫	13	14	⑮	16	17	⑱	19	20
㉑	22	23	㉔	25	26	㉗	28	29	㉚

Lexi should change the bedding on every multiple of 5.

1	2	3	4	5	6	7	8	9	10
11	12	13	14	15	16	17	18	19	20
21	22	23	24	25	26	27	28	29	30

Both jobs need to be done on each day that is a multiple of **both** 3 and 5.

1	2	③	4	5	⑥	7	8	⑨	10
11	⑫	13	14	⑮	16	17	⑱	19	20
㉑	22	23	㉔	25	26	㉗	28	29	㉚

> I can see that 15 and 30 are common multiples of 3 and 5.

Lexi will need to do both jobs on day 15 and day 30.

b) 30 is a multiple of 2, 3 and 5.

1	2	③	4	5	⑥	7	8	⑨	10
11	⑫	13	14	⑮	16	17	⑱	19	20
㉑	22	23	㉔	25	26	㉗	28	29	㉚

> I marked the multiples like this:
> multiples of 2 ☐
> multiples of 3 ○
> multiples of 5 ▨

Lexi will need to do all three jobs on day 30.

Think together

1 Aki visits his gran every 4 days. Aki's mum visits her every 6 days.

On which days do they both visit Gran?

1	2	3	4	5	6	7	8	9	10
11	12	13	14	15	16	17	18	19	20
21	22	23	24	25	26	27	28	29	30
31	32	33	34	35	36	37	38	39	40
41	42	43	44	45	46	47	48	49	50

Common multiples of 4 and 6 are ⬜, ⬜, ⬜, ...

They both visit Gran on days _____ .

2 Emma has cubes that are 5 cm tall. Ambika has cubes that are 12 cm tall.

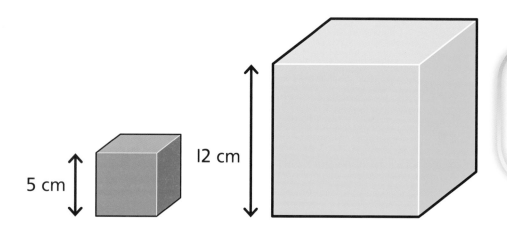

12 cm

5 cm

I will think about common multiples.

I think there is more than one solution.

They each make a tower. The two towers are equal in height. How tall could the towers be?

The towers could be ⬜ cm tall.

3 What do you notice about all the common multiples of 20 and 100?

4 Max and Jamilla are discussing common factors and common multiples.

| 10 | 25 |

I can list all the common factors of 10 and 25, so I must be able to list all the common multiples of 10 and 25.

I do not think it's possible to list all the common multiples, because the list goes on forever. Common factors and common multiples are different ideas.

Max

Jamilla

a) Do you agree with Max or Jamilla?

b) How could you describe the common multiples of 10 and 25, without listing them all?

91

Recognising prime numbers up to 100

Discover

1 a) Can Isla make more arrays if she uses 17 counters?

b) How many arrays can you make using 13 or 19 counters?

Share

a) If Isla tries to make an array using 17 counters with 2 rows or 3 rows or 4 rows, the rows cannot be equal.

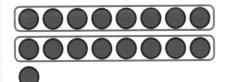

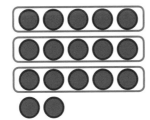

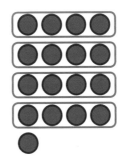

$17 \div 2 = 8 \text{ r } 1$

$17 \div 3 = 5 \text{ r } 2$

$17 \div 4 = 4 \text{ r } 1$

$17 \div 5 = 3 \text{ r } 2$

Only two different arrays are possible using 17 counters:

1 row of 17 because $17 \div 1 = 17$

17 rows of 1 because $17 \div 17 = 1$

Isla cannot make more arrays using Aki's counter.

> I remember that 17 is a prime number. It leaves a remainder when I divide it by any number other than 1 or itself.

b) 13 and 19 are both prime numbers, so you can only make two arrays for each.

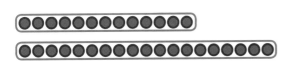

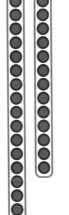

> Prime numbers have exactly 2 factors.

Think together

1 Mo makes these rows from cubes.

He says they prove that 11 and 21 are both prime numbers.

Do you agree?

I will check the factors for each number.

2 Alex thinks she has circled all the prime numbers up to 50.

Miss Hall has told her she has made two mistakes.

What are the two mistakes?

Could I be a prime number?

1	2	3	4	5	6	7	8	9	10
11	12	13	14	15	16	17	18	19	20
21	22	23	24	25	26	27	28	29	30
31	32	33	34	35	36	37	38	39	40
41	42	43	44	45	46	47	48	49	50

3 Bella and Richard are discussing how to find out if 97 is a prime number.

I can check if a number is prime by dividing by 2, then 3, then 4, to see if there is always a remainder.

But how do you know when to stop checking?

Bella

Richard

a) Will Bella's method work?

When should she stop checking?

b) Look at these numbers. Which numbers are prime?

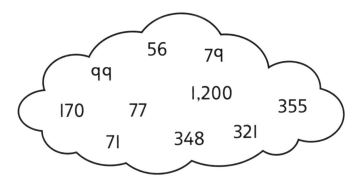

56   79
99
          1,200
170   77   355
   71   348   321

I can tell just by looking at some of these that they are not prime numbers.

Numbers that are not prime are called composite numbers.

95

→ Practice book 6A p67

Squares and cubes

Discover

What is the largest solid cube you can make with 16 small cubes?

I can make a large solid cube using all 16 small cubes, because 4 × 4 = 16.

Lee

① **a)** Is Lee correct? Can he make a large solid cube using all 16 small cubes?

b) What is the largest solid cube Lee can make? How many more cubes would he need to make the next largest cube?

Share

a) 4 × 4 makes a square number, not a cube number.

You can also write $4^2 = 16$.

The ^{2} tells you the number is squared.

The 4 is multiplied by itself.

$4^2 = 4 \times 4$

4 × 4 = 16

16 is a square number.

Lee has made a mistake. He cannot make one large solid cube using all 16 small cubes.

b) The largest solid cube that Lee can make uses 8 small cubes.

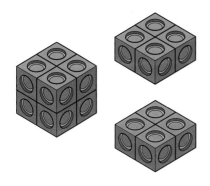

8 is a cube number.

A ^{3} tells you a number is cubed.

$2 \times 2 \times 2 = 2^3 = 8$.

You can calculate the total in layers. There are 2 layers of 2 × 2.

The next largest cube will be 3 × 3 × 3.

3^3 is 3 × 3 × 3 = 27.

There are 3 layers of 3 × 3.

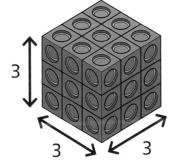

Lee will need 11 more small cubes to make the next largest cube.

Think together

1 Complete each calculation and match it to the correct diagram.

a)

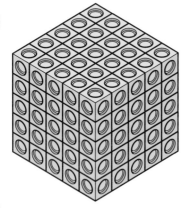

c)

b)

d)

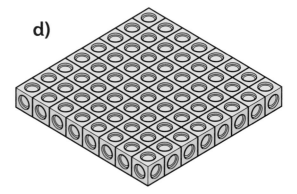

$\boxed{} \times \boxed{} = \boxed{}^2 = 25$

$\boxed{} \times \boxed{} \times \boxed{} = \boxed{}^3 = 125$

$\boxed{} \times \boxed{} = \boxed{}^2 = 64$

$\boxed{} \times \boxed{} \times \boxed{} = \boxed{}^3 = 64$

That is strange. I wonder if 64 can be both a square number and a cube number.

2 Luis is trying to work out if 6^2 is greater than 4^3.

I know 4^3 is $4 \times 3 = 12$.
6^2 must be 12 as well.
So they are equal.

Luis

Explain his mistake and show the correct working.

3 Use or create a multiplication grid like the one below.

Use counters to cover all the square numbers.

Do you notice a pattern?

×	1	2	3	4	5	6	7	8	9	10	11	12
1	1	2	3	4	5	6	7	8	9	10	11	12
2	2	4	6	8	10	12	14	16	18	20	22	24
3	3	6	9	12	15	18	21	24	27	30	33	36
4	4	8	12	16	20	24	28	32	36	40	44	48
5	5	10	15	20	25	30	35	40	45	50	55	60
6	6	12	18	24	30	36	42	48	54	60	66	72
7	7	14	21	28	35	42	49	56	63	70	77	84
8	8	16	24	32	40	48	56	64	72	80	88	96
9	9	18	27	36	45	54	63	72	81	90	99	108
10	10	20	30	40	50	60	70	80	90	100	110	120
11	11	22	33	44	55	66	77	88	99	110	121	132
12	12	24	36	48	60	72	84	96	108	120	132	144

I wonder why there is not a pattern for cube numbers on this grid.

Maybe the grid needs to be extended beyond 12 × 12! I wonder how many rows and columns I would need so I can find 5^3.

99

→ **Practice book 6A p70**

Order of operations

Discover

Represent this calculation using equipment:

$$3 + 5 \times 2 = \underline{\quad}$$

Ebo

Lexi

1 **a)** Explain why Ebo and Lexi have produced different answers.

b) Who is correct?

Share

a) Ebo and Lexi have performed the calculation **3 + 5 × 2** in different orders. Ebo has worked from left to right.

First, he did 3 + 5.   Then he multiplied the result by 2.   His answer is 16.

Lexi worked in a different order.

First, she showed 5 × 2.   Then, she added the result to 3.   Her answer is 13.

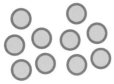

b) If there is a mixture of addition and multiplication, you should work out the multiplication first.

It is important that we all follow the same **order of operations** so we do not confuse each other with different solutions to the same calculation!

The correct answer is 13. Lexi is correct.

Think together

1 Look at these two ways of interpreting 3 × 5 – 2. Which is correct?

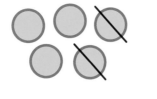
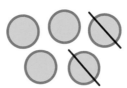

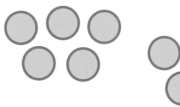

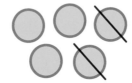

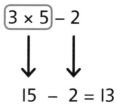

$3 \times \boxed{5 - 2}$

$3 \times 3 = 9$

$\boxed{3 \times 5} - 2$

$15 - 2 = 13$

2 Discuss how to solve each of these.

a) 100 – 25 × 2

b) 11 × 2 + 3 × 11

One of these has three operations. I will work out the multiplications first.

3 **a)** Work out these calculations.

$25 + 100 \div 4 = \boxed{}$

$\boxed{} = 500 \div 10 - 5$

I know what to do if there is a mixture of multiplication and addition or subtraction, but what about division?

b) Work out $2 \times 15 \div 3 = \boxed{}$ in different orders.

$\boxed{2 \times 15} \div 3$

$\boxed{} \div 3 = \boxed{}$

$2 \times \boxed{15 \div 3}$

$2 \times \boxed{} = \boxed{}$

What do you notice?

I wonder if the same thing always happens if you multiply and divide in one calculation.

What if the division is written before the multiplication, as in $10 \div 5 \times 2$?

103

→ **Practice book 6A p73**

Brackets

Discover

I have to check the tyres on 16 lorries today. Each cab has 4 wheels. Each trailer has 6 wheels.

1 **a)** The mechanic wants to work out how many tyres she needs to check.

She writes down $4 + 6 \times 16 = 160$.

Is her written calculation correct?

b) Another mechanic works out how many tyres are on 16 cabs and then how many tyres are on 16 trailers. He adds the two answers.

Show his method using a bar model and write the calculation for each step.

Share

a) The mechanic finds the total number of tyres on one cab and one trailer, then multiplies by 16 (the number of lorries).

The total number of tyres is $10 \times 16 = 160$.

The mechanic has the correct total, but her written calculation is incorrect. It gives an answer of 100.

$4 + 6 \times 16$

$4 + \boxed{6 \times 16}$

$4 + \quad 96 \quad = 100$

Sometimes a problem requires us to solve operations in a different order. Brackets show which parts of a calculation are worked out together first.

$(4 + 6) \times 16$

$\boxed{4 + 6} \times 16$

$10 \quad \times 16 = 160$

b) This bar model shows the second mechanic's method.

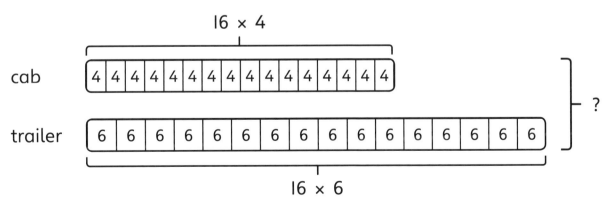

16×4

cab | 4 4 4 4 4 4 4 4 4 4 4 4 4 4 4 4

trailer | 6 6 6 6 6 6 6 6 6 6 6 6 6 6 6 6

16×6

?

This can be written as: $16 \times 4 + 16 \times 6$

$\boxed{16 \times 4} + \boxed{16 \times 6}$

$64 \quad + \quad 96 \quad = 160$

Think together

MENU

Veggie burger: £7·50

Fries: £3·50

1 A family orders 4 meals of veggie burger and fries.

Add brackets to the calculation to show the cost of 4 lots of veggie burger and fries.

Work out the value inside the brackets and then find the total.

4   × £7·50 + £3·50 = ▢

▢ × ▢ = ▢

> I wonder if I will get the same answer if I work out 4 × £7·50 then 4 × £3·50.

2 Complete these pairs of calculations.

a) $(15 - 5) \times 3 = $ ▢

$15 - (5 \times 3) = $ ▢

b) ▢ $= (15 + 5) \times (15 - 5)$

▢ $= 15 + (5 \times 15) - 5$

3 **a)** Add brackets to make each of these calculations correct.

$$4 + 4 \times 4 \div 4 = 8$$

$$4 + 4 \times 4 \div 4 = 5$$

I will try putting brackets around three of the 4s.

b) Choose operations to make these calculations correct.

$(4 \bigcirc 4) \bigcirc (4 \bigcirc 4) = 2$

$4 \bigcirc (4 \bigcirc 4) \bigcirc 4 = 28$

I wonder if I can write calculations that make all the numbers from 1 to 20 using just four 4s.

Maybe if I write two of the 4s as 44 I can make more of the numbers!

→ Practice book 6A p76

Mental calculations ❶

Discover

❶ **a)** Holly buys 5 loaves of bread. She pays with £5.

How much change does she receive?

b) Toshi buys yoghurt, bread and cereal. He pays with a £10 note.

How much change does he receive?

Share

a) £0·99 is 1p less than £1. This can be solved with a mental method.

Loaves	Pay with	Change	Cost
1			£1 − 1p = £0·99
2			£2 − 2p = £1·98
3			£3 − 3p = £2·97
4			£4 − 4p = £3·96
5			£5 − 5p = £4·95

Holly spends £4·95 in total. She receives 5p change.

b)

```
  2 9 9
    9 9
+ 3 9 9
───────

───────
```

First I need to work out how much Toshi spends in total. I will try column addition.

This needs a lot of exchanges. Perhaps there is a better method.

I can see a mental method.

£2·99 is 1p less than £3.

£0·99 is 1p less than £1.

£3·99 is very close to £4 too.

£3 + £1 + £4 = £8

If Toshi pays with £8, he will get 3p change.

−3p

£7·95　£7·96　£7·97　£7·98　£7·99　£8·00

Toshi spends £7·97.

From £10 he receives £2·03 change.

Think together

1 A cereal bar costs 45p. Zac wants to buy 9 cereal bars. He knows three different methods to find the total cost.

a) Which of these methods best suits a mental calculation?

```
    4   5           4   5
  ×     9           4   5
  ───────           4   5
  ───────           4   5
                    4   5
                    4   5
                    4   5
                    4   5
                  + 4   5
                  ───────
                  ───────
```

10 × 45p

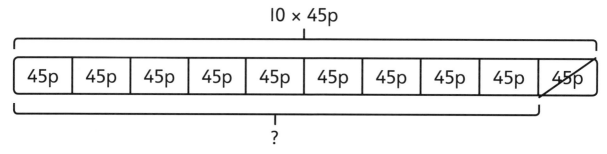

?

b) What is the total cost?

2 Calculate each of these mentally.

a) 19p + 29p + 39p

b) £10 − (3 × £0·99)

I think I may need to do more than one step to solve each calculation.

I will solve them mentally, then check with a written method.

3 **a)** Discuss whether these can be solved mentally or whether they are more suited to written methods.

> 7 × 25 g – 50 g
>
> (14 mm × 5) + (6 mm × 5)
>
> 10 m – (5 × 95 cm)

These look like they have mixed operations. I will use written methods because they need two steps.

I think these might suit mental methods.

It helps me to draw a bar model or a picture sometimes.

I think there are different ways to solve 7 × 25 – 50 mentally.

I will show both my ideas.

b) Think of a word problem to match each calculation.

!!!

→ **Practice book 6A p79**

Mental calculations ❷

Discover

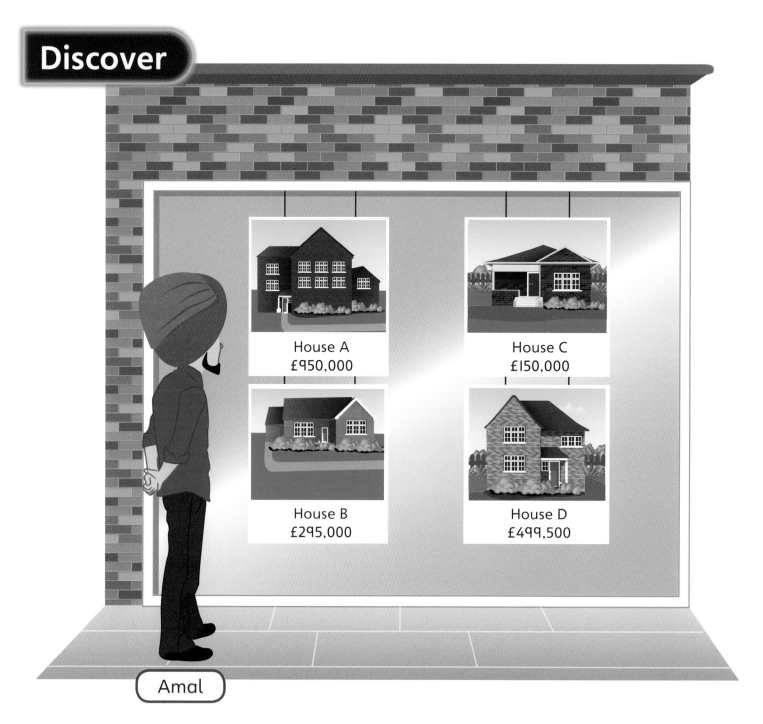

House A
£950,000

House C
£150,000

House B
£295,000

House D
£499,500

Amal

1 **a)** The estate agent reduces the prices of House B and House D by £10,000. What methods can you use to work out the new costs?

b) What is the difference in price between the most expensive house and the least expensive house?

Share

a) This requires two subtractions.

> I wrote a column subtraction to work out the new cost of House B.

House B

$$
\begin{array}{r}
2\,9\,5,0\,0\,0 \\
-\quad 1\,0,0\,0\,0 \\
\hline
2\,8\,5,0\,0\,0
\end{array}
$$

> To work out the new cost of House D, I subtracted 10,000 mentally by thinking about which digit will change.

House D

HTh	TTh	Th	H	T	O
4	9	9	5	0	0

The ten thousands digit will reduce by 1.

£499,500 – £10,000 is £489,500.

The mental method works well for these numbers.

b) The difference in price is 950,000 – 150,000.

That is, 950 thousands – 150 thousands.

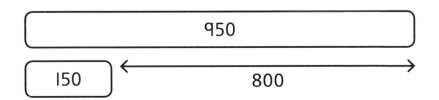

950

150   ←———————————→
              800

950 – 150 = 800, so the difference must be 800 thousands.

House A is £800,000 more expensive than House C.

Think together

1   Amal has saved half of the money for House C.

How much has he saved?

House C
£150,000

Now I will think about it as
150 thousands. I can work
out half of 150 mentally.

2   House A was £950,000 but it increases to one million pounds.

By how much does it increase?

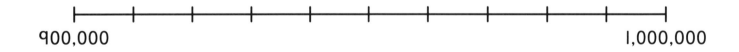

900,000   1,000,000

3   Calculate these mentally.

a)   One thousand more than two hundred and fifty-five thousand.

b)   25,000 less than 1,475,000.

c)   Half of one hundred thousand.

d)   What do you need to add to 499,000 to make a million?

4 Luis has been given this exercise.

Calculate these.

1,000 – 10

10,000 – 10

100,000 – 100

10,000,000 – 10,000

He tries some of the subtractions using a column method, but has to exchange many columns.

Can you think of a method using mental reasoning or jottings?

I wonder if a number line would show these.

I will use the inverse operation and change them into missing number problems like this:

1,000 = ☐ + 10

115

Reasoning from known facts

Discover

Fill in the three missing whole numbers in this calculation.

Each number is less than 10.

$$\square \times \square \times \square = 270$$

I know 3 × 9 = 27. I wonder if that could help.

I is a factor of every number and 2 must be a factor because 270 is even. Could I or 2 be a missing number?

Zac

Alex

1 a) Can Alex use 1 or 2 as a missing number?

b) Use Zac's idea to find a solution to the problem.

Share

a) If Alex uses 1, then the calculation will look like this:

$$1 \times \boxed{? \times ?} = 270$$

↓ ↓

$$1 \times 270 = 270$$

So, the result of multiplying the other two unknown numbers has to be 270.

If she uses 2, then the calculation will look like this:

$$2 \times \boxed{? \times ?} = 270$$

↓ ↓

$$2 \times 135 = 270$$

So, the result of multiplying the other two unknown numbers has to be 135.

Each number has to be less than 10, so $9 \times 9 = 81$ is the maximum possible answer.

This means Alex cannot use 1 or 2 to solve the problem.

b) $$3 \times \boxed{? \times ?} = 270$$

↓

$$3 \times 90 = 270$$

Zac cannot make 90 by multiplying two 1-digit numbers.

$$\boxed{? \times ?} \times 9 = 270$$

↓

$$30 \times 9 = 270$$

Zac can make 30 using two 1-digit numbers: $5 \times 6 = 30$.

The problem can be solved as $5 \times 6 \times 9 = 270$.

Think together

1 Can you use the fact shown in the box to work out 6 × 65 or 65 × 30 mentally?

$$3 \times 65 = 195$$

a) 6 × 65 = 2 × ⬚3 × 65⬚

6 × 65 = 2 × ⬚ = ⬚

b) 65 × 30 = ⬚65 × 3⬚ × 10

65 × 30 = ⬚ × 10 = ⬚

2 a) Can you use the fact that 3 × 65 = 195 to work out 4 × 65?

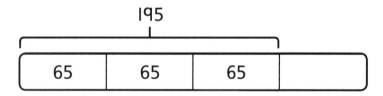

195

| 65 | 65 | 65 | |

> I think it will help to draw a diagram for 4 × 65.

b) Can you also use 3 × 65 = 195 to work out 66 × 3?

> I wonder if a bar model would help me to work out 66 × 3.
>
> I think I need 65 bars of 3.

3 Jamie is creating a mind map of facts she can work out from the known fact shown in the box.

1,870 ÷ 11 = 170

Explain how to use this division fact to work out the related multiplication facts.

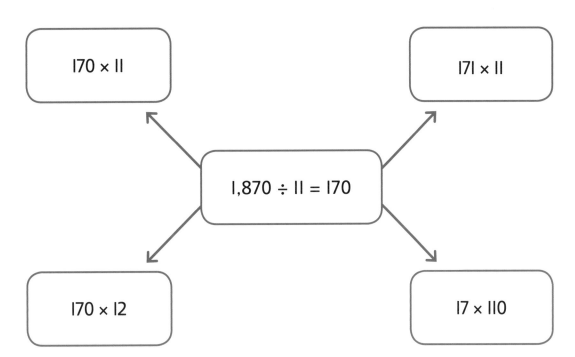

170 × 11

171 × 11

1,870 ÷ 11 = 170

170 × 12

17 × 110

I can think of even more related facts!

→ **Practice book 6A p85**

End of unit check

1 Complete the sentence.

'12 is a common factor of ...'

A 3 and 4   B 100 and 120   C 24 and 60   D 36

2 Which of these is **not** a prime number?

A 47   B 2   C 97   D 27

3 Which picture represents 2^3?

A

C

B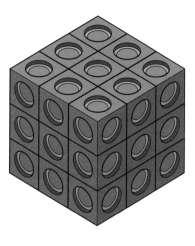

D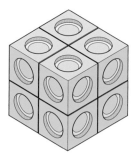

4 Which calculation is represented?

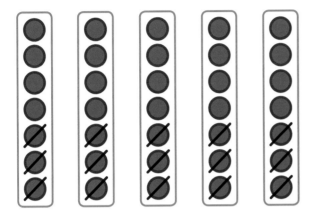

A 7 − 3 × 5   B 7 × 5 − 3   C 7 − (3 × 5)   D (7 − 3) × 5

5 What is one hundred less than two million?

A 1,900,000   B 1,999,900   C 199,900   D 1,900,900

6 2,332 ÷ 11 = 212

Explain how to use this fact to find 212 × 13.

→ Practice book 6A p88

Unit 4
Fractions ❶

In this unit we will …

⚡ Simplify fractions

⚡ Compare and order fractions

⚡ Add and subtract fractions including mixed numbers

⚡ Solve problems involving adding and subtracting fractions

Do you remember how to add two fractions where one denominator is a multiple of another?

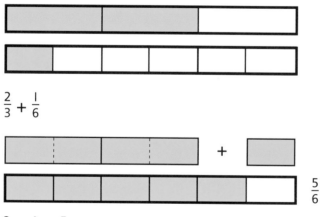

$\frac{2}{3} + \frac{1}{6}$

$\frac{5}{6}$

$\frac{2}{3} + \frac{1}{6} = \frac{5}{6}$

We will need some maths words.
Do you know what they all mean?

numerator   denominator

common denominator   common factor   equivalent

simplify   simplest form   factor

highest common factor   lowest common multiple (LCM)

compare   order   ascending   descending

proper fraction   improper fraction

mixed number   convert

lowest common denominator   equivalent

We also need to be able to find
where a fraction is on a number line.

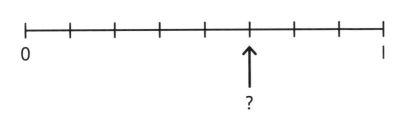

Simplifying fractions ①

Discover

Player 1: Get the cows into the pen.

Score
2 out of 4

Lee

Bella

① **a)** Bella gets 2 cows into the pen before the time runs out.

What is her score? Give your answer as a fraction in its simplest form.

b) Lee gets 9 of the 12 sheep into the pen.

What is his score? Give your answer as a fraction in its simplest form.

Share

a)

To find a fraction's simplest form we divide the numerator and the denominator by a **common factor**.

Bella's score is 2 out of 4.

We can write this fraction as $\frac{2}{4}$.

$\div 2$

$\frac{2}{4} = \frac{1}{2}$

$\div 2$

I divided the numerator and denominator by 2 because 2 is a common factor of 2 and 4.

$\frac{2}{4}$ can be simplified to $\frac{1}{2}$. Bella's score is $\frac{1}{2}$.

b) Lee gets $\frac{9}{12}$ of the sheep in the pen.

We can divide the numerator and the denominator by 3 because 3 is a common factor of 9 and 12.

$\div 3$

$\frac{9}{12} = \frac{3}{4}$

$\div 3$

These fractions represent the same amount, but one is written in its simplest form.

Lee's score is $\frac{3}{4}$.

Think together

1. Bella and Lee play some more rounds of the game. What scores do they get? Use the diagrams to help you simplify the fractions.

a) Bella gets 4 out of 6 sheep in the pen.

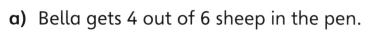
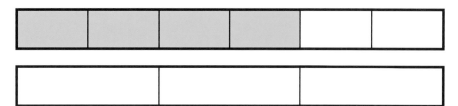

$$\frac{4}{6} = \frac{\boxed{}}{3}$$

$\div 2$

$\div 2$

b) Lee gets 5 out of 10 cows in the pen.

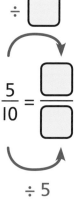

$$\frac{5}{10} = \frac{\boxed{}}{\boxed{}}$$

$\div \boxed{}$

$\div 5$

c) Bella gets 9 out of 15 geese in the pen.

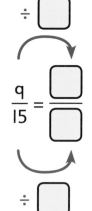

$$\frac{9}{15} = \frac{\boxed{}}{\boxed{}}$$

$\div \boxed{}$

$\div \boxed{}$

2 Simplify these fractions.

a) $\dfrac{6}{8}$

b) $\dfrac{10}{100}$

c) $\dfrac{7}{7}$

3 a) Use your knowledge of equivalent fractions to find the missing numbers.

CHALLENGE

× 2

$$\frac{5}{6} = \frac{10}{\boxed{}}$$

× 2

$$\frac{3}{10} = \frac{15}{\boxed{}}$$

Equivalent means equal to.

b) Fill in the missing numbers to make the simplified fractions correct.

$$\frac{15 + 5}{29 + 6} = \frac{\boxed{}}{\boxed{}}$$

$$\frac{\boxed{} + 19}{30} = \frac{5}{6}$$

$$\frac{25 - \boxed{}}{28} = \frac{3}{4}$$

$$\frac{\boxed{} + 15}{20} = \frac{4}{\boxed{}}$$

I remember how to find equivalent fractions. I need to multiply the numerator and denominator by the same number.

127

Simplifying fractions ❷

Discover

❶ **a)** What fraction of the people are children?

Simplify your answer.

b) How many roller coaster carriages are full?

Simplify your answer.

Share

a) 12 children: factors of 12 are 1, 2, 3, 4, ⑥ and 12

18 people: factors of 18 are 1, 2, 3, ⑥, 9, 18

The **highest common factor** of 12 and 18 is 6. This is the highest number that divides into both 12 and 18.

Divide the numerator and denominator by 6. $\frac{12}{18} = \frac{2}{3}$ ÷ 6 ... ÷ 6

I did it a different way. I know that 12 and 18 can both be divided by 2 so I started by doing that. I then noticed I could divide the answer by 3.

Divide the numerator and denominator by 2. $\frac{12}{18} = \frac{6}{9}$ ÷ 2 ... ÷ 2

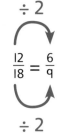

6 and 9 have a common factor of 3.
Divide the numerator and denominator by 3.

$\frac{6}{9} = \frac{2}{3}$ ÷ 3 ... ÷ 3

$\frac{2}{3}$ of the people are children.

b)

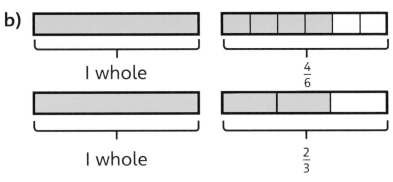

I whole

$\frac{4}{6}$

I whole

$\frac{2}{3}$

We know we have simplified fully when we cannot divide the numerator and denominator by any other number apart from 1.

I carriage is full and the other is $\frac{4}{6}$ full.

To simplify $1\frac{4}{6}$ we keep the whole number the same and simplify the fraction.

$1\frac{4}{6}$ simplifies to $1\frac{2}{3}$.

$1\frac{2}{3}$ roller coaster carriages are full.

Think together

 a) Olivia wants to go on the ghost train. Three of the carriages are full. In the remaining carriage, 8 out of 10 seats are taken.

Simplify $3\frac{8}{10}$

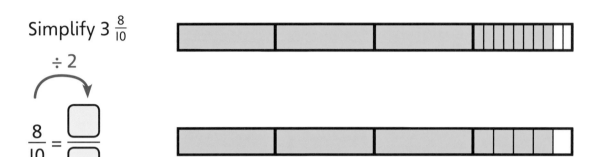

$\div 2$

$\frac{8}{10} = \frac{\square}{\square}$

$\div 2$

So $3\frac{8}{10} = \square\frac{\square}{\square}$

b) When she gets off the train after her ride, she counts 25 people waiting. Each carriage has 10 seats.

How many carriages will be full? Simplify your answer.

$\frac{25}{10} = \square\frac{\square}{10} = \square\frac{\square}{\square}$

2 Some children are trying to fully simplify $16\frac{8}{24}$.

They all use a different method. Which children have used correct methods? Explain how you know.

> The highest common factor of 16, 8 and 24 is 8, so I divided all the numbers by 8.

Olivia

> I kept the whole number the same and divided the numerator and denominator by the highest common factor of 8.

Lexi

> I kept the whole number the same and divided the numerator and denominator by 4.

Isla

> I divided all the numbers by 2, then by 2 again, then by 2 again.

Amelia

> I divided the numerator and denominator by 2, then by 4, but kept the whole number the same.

Emma

CHALLENGE

3 Which is bigger:

$\frac{288}{160}$ or $\frac{9}{5}$?

Explain how you know.

> I will simplify the fractions before I compare them.

> I wonder what is the best way to simplify the fractions.

131

Fractions on a number line

Discover

Max

1 a) The ceiling on Max's side of the room drips $\frac{1}{4}$ litre of water every hour.

Max has already collected $\frac{1}{2}$ a litre of water in his jug.

How many litres of water will be in his jug after another 3 hours?

b) Max collects $5\frac{3}{4}$ litres of water in total. His dad collects $5\frac{4}{5}$ litres of water in total.

Use a number line to show who collected the most water.

Share

a) Max's jug contains $\frac{1}{2}$ litre of water to start with.

Starting from $\frac{1}{2}$ we can count up in quarters ($\frac{1}{4}$).

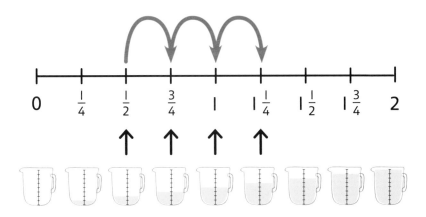

0    $\frac{1}{4}$ $\frac{1}{2}$ $\frac{3}{4}$ 1 $1\frac{1}{4}$ $1\frac{1}{2}$ $1\frac{3}{4}$ 2

> I counted up $\frac{1}{4}$ three times.

There will be $1\frac{1}{4}$ litres of water in Max's jug after another 3 hours.

b) Both amounts of water lie between 5 and 6.

We can compare number lines divided into quarters and fifths.

Max

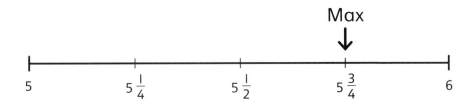

5    $5\frac{1}{4}$ $5\frac{1}{2}$ $5\frac{3}{4}$ 6

> I put my number lines together to help me compare.

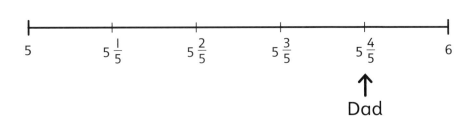

5    $5\frac{1}{5}$ $5\frac{2}{5}$ $5\frac{3}{5}$ $5\frac{4}{5}$ 6

Dad

$5\frac{4}{5}$ is bigger than $5\frac{3}{4}$ so Max's dad collected the most water.

Think together

1 Danny is running a bath. There are 2 litres of water in the bath already. It fills up at a rate of $\frac{1}{3}$ litre each second. How many litres are in the bath after 8 seconds?

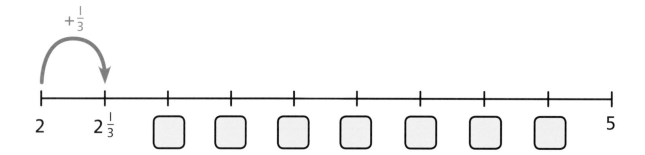

There are ⬜ $\frac{⬜}{⬜}$ litres of water in the bath after 8 seconds.

2 a) What numbers are missing from the number line?

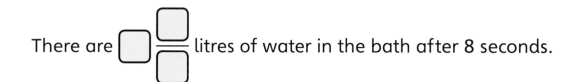

b) What numbers are missing from the number line?

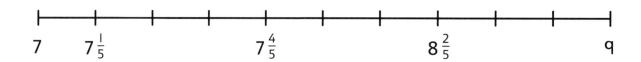

c) Danny is counting up from 1 to 3 in jumps of $\frac{2}{6}$. Complete the jumps and fill in the missing numbers.

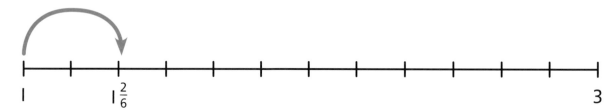

3

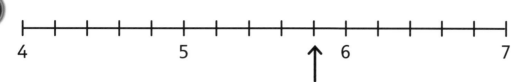

a) What number is the arrow pointing to?

b) What is $\frac{2}{5}$ **more** than the number the arrow is pointing to?

c) What is $\frac{1}{5}$ **less** than the number the arrow is pointing to?

d) What is 1 more than the number the arrow is pointing to?

4 a) Find where these numbers should go on the number line.

$2\frac{3}{10}$ $2\frac{1}{2}$ $2\frac{9}{10}$

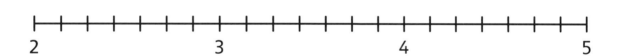

2   3

b) This sequence goes up by the same amount each time. Use the number line to help you work out the missing fractions.

$\boxed{}$, $3\frac{1}{7}$, $\boxed{}$, $\boxed{}$, $4\frac{3}{7}$, $\boxed{}$

2   3   4   5

I used the number line and looked at the gaps between the numbers.

135

→ Practice book 6A p96

Comparing and ordering fractions ❶

Discover

Group A   Group B

❶ **a)** Which group has a bigger fraction of people wearing glasses?

b) Some more people are in Group C. $\frac{2}{3}$ of the people in Group C are wearing glasses.

Which group now has the biggest fraction of people wearing glasses?

Share

a) We need to compare $\frac{3}{4}$ and $\frac{5}{8}$.

Group A

Group B

$\frac{3}{4}$ is equivalent to $\frac{6}{8}$.

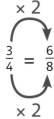

$$\overset{\times\,2}{\underset{\times\,2}{\frac{3}{4} = \frac{6}{8}}}$$

I found equivalent fractions for Group A so that I could compare $\frac{1}{8}$s.

$\frac{6}{8}$ is greater than $\frac{5}{8}$ so $\frac{3}{4}$ is greater than $\frac{5}{8}$.

Group A has a bigger fraction of people wearing glasses.

b) Now we need to compare $\frac{3}{4}$ and $\frac{2}{3}$.

Group A

Group C

Multiples of 4 are 4, 8, ⑫.

Multiples of 3 are 3, 6, 9, ⑫.

The lowest common multiple of 4 and 3 is 12 so we can find equivalent fractions with a denominator of 12.

$$\overset{\times\,3}{\underset{\times\,3}{\frac{3}{4} = \frac{9}{12}}} \qquad \overset{\times\,4}{\underset{\times\,4}{\frac{2}{3} = \frac{8}{12}}}$$

I needed to find equivalent fractions for both groups. To get the same denominator I found the **lowest common multiple (LCM)** of 4 and 3.

$\frac{9}{12} > \frac{8}{12}$ so $\frac{3}{4} > \frac{2}{3}$

Group A has the biggest fraction of people wearing glasses.

Think together

1 **a)** $\frac{5}{6}$ of Class A have brown hair. $\frac{2}{3}$ of Class B have brown hair. Which class has a bigger fraction of children with brown hair?

Class A

Class B

The LCM of 6 and 3 is ▢. $\frac{2}{3} = \frac{\Box}{6}$ $\frac{5}{6} \bigcirc \frac{\Box}{6}$ so $\frac{5}{6} \bigcirc \frac{2}{3}$.

Class ▢ has a bigger fraction of children with brown hair.

b) $\frac{1}{2}$ of Class A has a pet. $\frac{3}{8}$ of Class B have a pet.

Which class has a bigger fraction of children with a pet?

Class A

Class B

The LCM of 2 and 8 is ▢. $\frac{1}{2} = \frac{\Box}{\Box}$ $\frac{1}{2} \bigcirc \frac{3}{8}$

Class ▢ has a bigger fraction of children with a pet.

c) $\frac{3}{5}$ of Class A are girls. $\frac{2}{3}$ of Class B are girls.

Which class has a bigger fraction of girls?

The LCM of 5 and 3 is ▢.

$\frac{3}{5} = \frac{\Box}{\Box}$ $\frac{2}{3} = \frac{\Box}{\Box}$ $\frac{3}{5} \bigcirc \frac{2}{3}$

Class ▢ has a bigger fraction of girls.

138

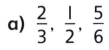 **2** Put each of these sets of fractions in order from smallest to biggest.

a) $\frac{2}{3}, \frac{1}{2}, \frac{5}{6}$

> I need to find the lowest common multiple of more than two numbers here. This will be the denominator that I need to use in order to compare.

b) $\frac{1}{2}, \frac{5}{12}, \frac{5}{6}, \frac{3}{4}$

c) $\frac{4}{5}, \frac{3}{10}, \frac{49}{50}, \frac{4}{4}, \frac{99}{100}$

3 Fill in the missing digits to make the statements correct.

CHALLENGE

a) $\frac{\boxed{}}{6}$ is bigger than $\frac{2}{3}$

d) $\frac{\boxed{}}{5} > \frac{1}{2} > \frac{\boxed{}}{10}$

b) $\frac{2}{5}$ is smaller than $\frac{\boxed{}}{15}$

e) $\frac{3}{8} < \frac{\boxed{}}{6}$

c) $\frac{1}{3} > \frac{\boxed{}}{4}$

f) $\frac{3}{\boxed{}} < \frac{\boxed{}}{3}$

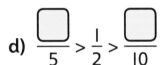

> I think some statements may have more than one answer.

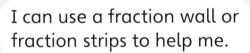

> I can use a fraction wall or fraction strips to help me.

139

Comparing and ordering fractions ❷

Discover

1 **a)** Does Bella's cat eat more than Jamie's cat each day?

b) Ebo's cat eats $\frac{11}{7}$ pouches of cat food each day.

Does Ebo's cat eat more than Bella's cat?

Share

a) Bella's cat

Jamie's cat

I need to compare $1\frac{3}{5}$ and $1\frac{2}{3}$. I think I only need to compare the fractions.

To compare $\frac{3}{5}$ and $\frac{2}{3}$ I need to find the **lowest common denominator**.

Multiples of 5 are 5, 10, ⑮.

Multiples of 3 are 3, 6, 9, 12, ⑮.

The lowest common denominator is 15.

$\frac{9}{15} < \frac{10}{15}$ so $\frac{3}{5} < \frac{2}{3}$

$1\frac{3}{5}$ is less than $1\frac{2}{3}$ so Bella's cat does not eat more than Jamie's cat each day.

b) We need to compare $1\frac{3}{5}$ and $\frac{11}{7}$.

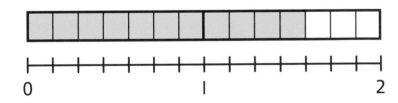

I converted $\frac{11}{7}$ to $1\frac{4}{7}$ so they are easier to compare.

The whole numbers are the same so we only need to compare $\frac{3}{5}$ and $\frac{4}{7}$.

The lowest common denominator is 35.

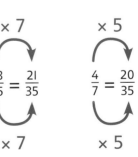

$\frac{21}{35} > \frac{20}{35}$ so $\frac{3}{5} > \frac{4}{7}$ so $1\frac{3}{5} > 1\frac{4}{7}$

$\frac{11}{7} < 1\frac{3}{5}$ so Ebo's cat does not eat more than Bella's cat.

Think together

1 a) Lexi's hamster eats $2\frac{3}{4}$ bowls of food each week. Her gerbil eats $2\frac{7}{12}$ bowls of food each week. Which animal eats more each week?

hamster

gerbil

$\frac{3}{4} = \dfrac{\boxed{}}{12}$

So $2\frac{3}{4} = 2\dfrac{\boxed{}}{12}$

$2\frac{3}{4} \bigcirc 2\frac{7}{12}$

Lexi's _____ eats more each week.

b) There are 8 carrots in a bag. Roxy the horse eats 27 carrots per week.

How many bags of carrots does she eat per week?

$\dfrac{\boxed{}}{8} = \boxed{}\dfrac{\boxed{}}{8}$

Roxy eats $\boxed{}\dfrac{\boxed{}}{\boxed{}}$ bags of carrots per week.

c) Mai the horse eats $3\frac{1}{2}$ bags of carrots per week.

Which horse eats more carrots per week?

$3\frac{1}{2} = 3\dfrac{\boxed{}}{8}$ $\boxed{}\dfrac{\boxed{}}{8} \bigcirc 3\dfrac{\boxed{}}{8}$

_____ eats more carrots per week.

2 Max has four fraction cards.

$5\frac{2}{7}$ $5\frac{10}{21}$ $5\frac{6}{14}$ $\frac{36}{7}$

Which fraction is the biggest?

Put the fractions in ascending order.

3 Jamilla has some fraction cards.

She selects the following fraction card.

$2\frac{3}{5}$

CHALLENGE

Which fraction cards are bigger than Jamilla's?

$1\frac{7}{10}$ $\frac{17}{10}$ $4\frac{1}{8}$ $2\frac{11}{20}$

$\frac{21}{4}$ $\frac{189}{724}$ $2\frac{2}{3}$ $2\frac{*}{20}$

Some of these are clearly bigger. I can tell by just looking.

The last card is bigger than Jamilla's number. I wonder what number could be missing.

→ **Practice book 6A p102**

Adding and subtracting fractions ①

Discover

I need to feed Hattie $\frac{2}{3}$ of a bale of hay in the morning and $\frac{1}{6}$ in the evening.

Hattie

Molly

① a) What fraction of a bale of hay does Hattie eat in a day?

b) Molly eats $\frac{1}{4}$ of a bale of hay less than Hattie per day.

What fraction of a bale of hay does Molly eat in a day?

Share

morning   evening

a)

$$\frac{2}{3} \qquad \frac{1}{6}$$

$$\frac{2}{3} + \frac{1}{6}$$

When adding or subtracting fractions, we need to find a common denominator.

Multiples of 3 are 3, ⑥.

A multiple of 6 is ⑥.

The lowest common multiple of 3 and 6 is 6.

I will find an equivalent fraction with a denominator of 6.

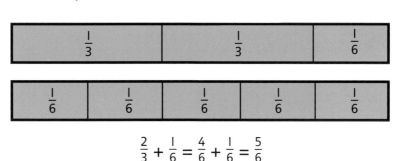

| $\frac{1}{3}$ | $\frac{1}{3}$ | $\frac{1}{6}$ |

| $\frac{1}{6}$ | $\frac{1}{6}$ | $\frac{1}{6}$ | $\frac{1}{6}$ | $\frac{1}{6}$ |

$$\frac{2}{3} + \frac{1}{6} = \frac{4}{6} + \frac{1}{6} = \frac{5}{6}$$

× 2

$$\frac{2}{3} = \frac{4}{6}$$

× 2

Hattie eats $\frac{5}{6}$ of a bale of hay in a day.

b) Molly eats $\frac{1}{4}$ of a bale less than Hattie.

Use the LCM of 6 and 4 to find a common denominator.

I need to subtract.

Multiples of 6 are 6, ⑫

Multiples of 4 are 4, 8, ⑫   The LCM is 12.

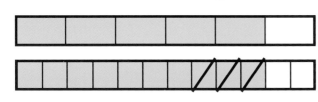

$$\frac{5}{6} - \frac{1}{4} = \frac{10}{12} - \frac{3}{12} = \frac{7}{12}$$

× 2   × 3

$$\frac{5}{6} = \frac{10}{12} \qquad \frac{1}{4} = \frac{3}{12}$$

× 2   × 3

Molly eats $\frac{7}{12}$ of a bale of hay in a day.

Think together

 a) Hector eats $\frac{1}{8}$ of a bale of hay in the morning and $\frac{3}{4}$ of a bale of hay in the evening. How much hay does he eat in a day?

The LCM of 8 and 4 is ☐. So $\frac{3}{4} = \dfrac{\boxed{}}{8}$

$\dfrac{1}{8} + \dfrac{\boxed{}}{\boxed{}} = \dfrac{\boxed{}}{\boxed{}}$

Hector eats ☐ of a bale of hay in a day.

b) Callie eats $\frac{2}{3}$ of a bale of hay. Scoobie eats $\frac{5}{9}$ less. How much does Scoobie eat?

The LCM of 3 and 9 is ☐. $\frac{2}{3} = \dfrac{\boxed{}}{\boxed{}}$

$\dfrac{\boxed{}}{\boxed{}} - \dfrac{\boxed{}}{\boxed{}} = \dfrac{\boxed{}}{\boxed{}}$

Scoobie eats ☐ of a bale of hay.

2 Work out $\frac{1}{6} + \frac{3}{8}$.

The LCM of 6 and 8 is ☐ .

$\frac{1}{6} = \dfrac{\boxed{}}{\boxed{}}$ $\frac{3}{8} = \dfrac{\boxed{}}{\boxed{}}$ $\dfrac{\boxed{}}{\boxed{}} + \dfrac{\boxed{}}{\boxed{}} = \dfrac{\boxed{}}{\boxed{}}$

3 Complete the following addition pyramids.

CHALLENGE

a)

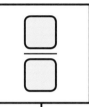

$\dfrac{\boxed{}}{\boxed{}}$

| $\frac{2}{5}$ | $\frac{1}{4}$ |

c)

$\dfrac{\boxed{}}{24}$

| $\dfrac{\boxed{}}{3}$ | $\frac{5}{8}$ |

b)

$\frac{11}{12}$

| $\frac{3}{4}$ | $\dfrac{\boxed{}}{6}$ |

d)

1

| $\frac{1}{5}$ | |

| $\frac{11}{100}$ | | |

I think I might need to subtract to find some of the missing fractions.

I think it would help to think about common denominators.

147

→ **Practice book 6A p105**

Adding and subtracting fractions ②

Discover

Circular
cycle route

$3\frac{2}{5}$ kilometres

1 **a)** On Saturday, Amelia cycles $3\frac{2}{5}$ kilometres with her dad.

On Sunday, she cycles $1\frac{1}{3}$ kilometres.

How many kilometres does Amelia cycle in total?

b) How many more kilometres does Amelia cycle on Saturday than on Sunday?

Share

a) Saturday

Sunday

Add the wholes: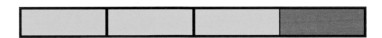

$3 + 1 = 4$

Add the parts:

$\frac{2}{5} + \frac{1}{3}$

Multiples of 5 are 5, 10, (15)

Multiples of 3 are 3, 6, 9, 12, (15)

The lowest common multiple is 15.

So

$\frac{2}{5} + \frac{1}{3} = \frac{6}{15} + \frac{5}{15} = \frac{11}{15}$

Amelia cycles $4 + \frac{11}{15} = 4\frac{11}{15}$ in total.

b) We need to subtract to find the difference.

$3\frac{2}{5} - 1\frac{1}{3}$

First subtract the wholes.

$3 - 1 = 2$

Then subtract the parts.

$\frac{2}{5} - \frac{1}{3} = \frac{6}{15} - \frac{5}{15} = \frac{1}{15}$

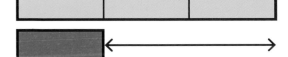

So Amelia cycles $2\frac{1}{15}$ more km on Saturday than on Sunday.

149

Think together

 a) Luis walks $2\frac{1}{4}$ kilometres on Saturday and $2\frac{3}{8}$ kilometres on Sunday.

Saturday

Sunday

How far does Luis walk in total?

Add the wholes: $2 + 2 = \boxed{}$

Add the parts: $\frac{1}{4} = \frac{\boxed{}}{8}$ $\frac{1}{4} + \frac{3}{8} = \frac{\boxed{}}{\boxed{}} + \frac{3}{8} = \frac{\boxed{}}{\boxed{}}$

$2\frac{1}{4} + 2\frac{3}{8} = \boxed{}\frac{\boxed{}}{\boxed{}}$ so Luis walks $\boxed{}\frac{\boxed{}}{\boxed{}}$ kilometres in total.

b) Jamie swims $5\frac{1}{2}$ lengths of a swimming pool.

Ambika swims $3\frac{2}{5}$ lengths of the swimming pool.

How many more lengths does Jamie swim than Ambika?

$\boxed{} - \boxed{} = \boxed{}$

$\frac{1}{2} = \frac{\boxed{}}{\boxed{}}$ $\frac{2}{5} = \frac{\boxed{}}{\boxed{}}$ $\frac{1}{2} - \frac{2}{5} = \frac{\boxed{}}{\boxed{}} - \frac{\boxed{}}{\boxed{}} = \frac{\boxed{}}{\boxed{}}$

$5\frac{1}{2} - 3\frac{2}{5} = \boxed{}\frac{\boxed{}}{\boxed{}} =$ so Jamie swims $\boxed{}\frac{\boxed{}}{\boxed{}}$ more lengths than Ambika.

2 Find the missing values.

a)

?	
$9\frac{1}{6}$	$7\frac{5}{8}$

b)

$4\frac{2}{3}$	
?	$\frac{2}{7}$

3 Richard's dad has a model railway, with a train track $2\frac{3}{4}$ metres long.

He buys a second train track.

This train track is $\frac{3}{5}$ metres shorter than the first one.

The tracks are put together to make a longer track.

How long is the new train track?

CHALLENGE

I think I need to do an addition and subtraction in this calculation.

I only have two fractions though.

→ Practice book 6A p108

Adding fractions

Discover

There are $2\frac{3}{4}$ tonnes of carrots on one trailer and $1\frac{1}{2}$ tonnes on the other.

1 a) What is the total weight of carrots the farmer has harvested so far?

b) A supermarket orders 5 tonnes of carrots.

The farmer harvests another $\frac{4}{5}$ tonnes of carrots from a different field.

Has the farmer harvested enough carrots to fulfil the order?

Share

a) We need to find $2\frac{3}{4} + 1\frac{1}{2}$.

Method 1

Add the wholes: $2 + 1 = 3$

Add the parts : $\frac{3}{4} + \frac{1}{2} = \frac{3}{4} + \frac{2}{4} = \frac{5}{4}$

$\frac{5}{4} = 1\frac{1}{4}$

So $2\frac{3}{4} + 1\frac{1}{4} = 3 + 1\frac{1}{4} = 4\frac{1}{4}$

> I made the improper fraction into a mixed number and then put the answers together.

Method 2

$2 = \frac{11}{4}$ $\qquad$ $1\frac{1}{2} = \frac{3}{2} = \frac{6}{4}$

So $2\frac{3}{4} + 1\frac{1}{2} = \frac{11}{4} + \frac{6}{4}$

$\qquad = \frac{17}{4} = 4\frac{1}{4}$

> I changed the mixed numbers to improper fractions first, then added them together.

The total weight of carrots the farmer has harvested so far is $4\frac{1}{4}$ tonnes.

b) Now we need to add $4\frac{1}{4} + \frac{4}{5}$.

Add the wholes: $4 + 0 = 4$

Add the parts: $\frac{1}{4} + \frac{4}{5} = \frac{5}{20} + \frac{16}{20} = \frac{21}{20} = 1\frac{1}{20}$

So $4\frac{1}{4} + \frac{4}{5} = 4 + 1\frac{1}{20} = 5\frac{1}{20}$.

$5\frac{1}{20}$ tonnes > 5 tonnes so the farmer has harvested enough carrots to fulfil the order.

Think together

1 Calculate $1\frac{2}{3} + 2\frac{1}{2}$.

a) Method 1

Add the wholes: $1 + 2 = \square$

Add the parts: $\frac{2}{3} + \frac{1}{2} = \frac{\square}{\square} + \frac{\square}{\square} = \frac{\square}{\square}$

$\frac{\square}{\square} = \square\frac{\square}{\square}$

Add them together: $1\frac{2}{3} + 2\frac{1}{2} = \square + \square\frac{\square}{\square} = \square\frac{\square}{\square}$

b) Method 2

Change to improper fractions: $1\frac{2}{3} = \frac{\square}{\square}$ $2\frac{1}{2} = \frac{\square}{\square}$

Now add the fractions: $\frac{\square}{3} + \frac{\square}{2} = \frac{\square}{\square} + \frac{\square}{\square} = \frac{\square}{\square}$

Change to a mixed number: $\frac{\square}{\square} = \square\frac{\square}{\square}$

2

chicken

mushroom

At a pizza buffet, 3 whole chicken pizzas and 7 slices were eaten.

Also, 4 whole mushroom pizzas and 5 slices were eaten.

How many pizzas were eaten altogether?

3 Here are some numbers.

CHALLENGE

$$7\frac{3}{4} \qquad 4\frac{2}{3} \qquad 3\frac{5}{6} \qquad 6\frac{7}{8} \qquad 27\frac{17}{24}$$

a) Isla adds two of the numbers together.

Her answer is $11\frac{13}{24}$.

Which two numbers did she choose?

b) What method would you use to add $7\frac{3}{4}$ and $27\frac{17}{24}$?

Explain your method.

I prefer to convert to improper fractions.

I am not sure what is the best method.

155

→ **Practice book 6A p111**

Subtracting fractions

Discover

I wonder how many more cups of cherries I need. I need to find $3\frac{1}{3} - 1\frac{1}{2}$.

I cannot find $3\frac{1}{3} - 1\frac{1}{2}$ because $\frac{1}{3}$ is less than $\frac{1}{2}$.

Isla

$3\frac{1}{3}$ cups cherries
$\frac{2}{3}$ cups sugar
$1\frac{1}{2}$ tbsp cornflour
$3\frac{1}{2}$ tbsp milk
1 sheet pastry.

$1\frac{1}{2}$ cups of cherries

Max

You can do the subtraction if you change both numbers to improper fractions.

1 a) Is Max correct?

b) Show how Isla's method will give you the answer to $3\frac{1}{3} - 1\frac{1}{2}$.

Share

a)

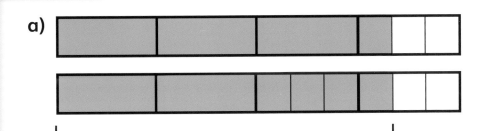

$$3\frac{1}{3} = 2\frac{4}{3}$$

Subtract the wholes: $2 - 1 = 1$

The lowest common multiple of 2 and 3 is 6.

Subtract the parts: $\frac{4}{3} - \frac{1}{2} = \frac{8}{6} - \frac{3}{6} = \frac{5}{6}$

$1 + \frac{5}{6} = 1\frac{5}{6}$

Max is not correct - he can do the subtraction. He needs $1\frac{5}{6}$ more cups of cherries.

> I needed to find $3\frac{1}{3} - 1\frac{1}{2}$. I rewrote $3\frac{1}{3}$ as $2\frac{4}{3}$ to make the fraction part bigger than $\frac{1}{2}$ so it was easier to subtract.

b)

$3\frac{1}{3} = \frac{10}{3}$

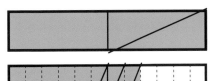

$1\frac{1}{2} = \frac{3}{2}$

$3\frac{1}{3} - 1\frac{1}{2}$ can be written as $\frac{10}{3} - \frac{3}{2}$

$\frac{10}{3} - \frac{3}{2} = \frac{20}{6} - \frac{9}{6} = \frac{11}{6}$

Change back to a mixed number: $\frac{11}{6} = 1\frac{5}{6}$

> I changed each number to an improper fraction.

Think together

1 **a)** Work out $4\frac{1}{3} - 2\frac{3}{4}$.

Use the diagram to help you explain the method.

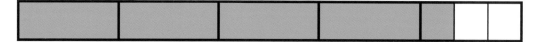

$4\frac{1}{3} = 3 + 1\frac{1}{3} = 3\frac{\boxed{}}{3}$

Subtract the wholes: $3 - 2 = \boxed{}$

The lowest common multiple of 3 and 4 is $\boxed{}$.

Subtract the parts:

$\frac{4}{3} - \frac{3}{4} = \frac{\boxed{}}{\boxed{}} - \frac{\boxed{}}{\boxed{}} = \frac{\boxed{}}{\boxed{}}$

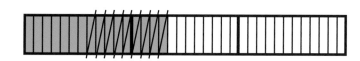

So $4\frac{1}{3} - 2\frac{3}{4} = \boxed{} + \frac{\boxed{}}{\boxed{}} = \boxed{}\frac{\boxed{}}{\boxed{}}$

b) Work out $3\frac{1}{5} - 1\frac{1}{2}$ by converting each mixed number to an improper fraction.

$3\frac{1}{5} = \frac{\boxed{}}{5}$ $1\frac{1}{2} = \frac{\boxed{}}{2}$ so $3\frac{1}{5} - 1\frac{1}{2}$ can be written as $\frac{\boxed{}}{5} - \frac{\boxed{}}{2}$

The lowest common multiple of 5 and 2 is $\boxed{}$.

Find a common denominator: $\frac{\boxed{}}{5} - \frac{\boxed{}}{2} = \frac{\boxed{}}{\boxed{}} - \frac{\boxed{}}{\boxed{}} = \frac{\boxed{}}{\boxed{}}$

Change back to a mixed number: $\frac{\boxed{}}{\boxed{}} = \boxed{}\frac{\boxed{}}{\boxed{}}$

2 It takes Jamilla $2\frac{1}{4}$ hours to complete a puzzle.

It takes Andy $\frac{2}{3}$ of an hour less.

How many hours does it take Andy to complete the puzzle?

3 **a)** Danny is working out $5\frac{3}{10} - 2\frac{5}{6}$.

He counts on a number line.

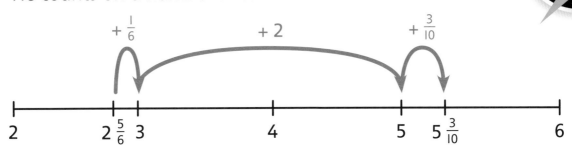

What answer will Danny get using this method?

> To find the answer using Danny's method, I will add the fractions and then the whole number.

b) Use Max's, Isla's and Danny's methods to work out $3\frac{1}{2} - 1\frac{7}{10}$ and $26\frac{1}{2} - 18\frac{4}{5}$.

> I wonder which method is most efficient when the whole numbers are big.

159

→ **Practice book 6A p114**

Problem solving – adding and subtracting fractions ❶

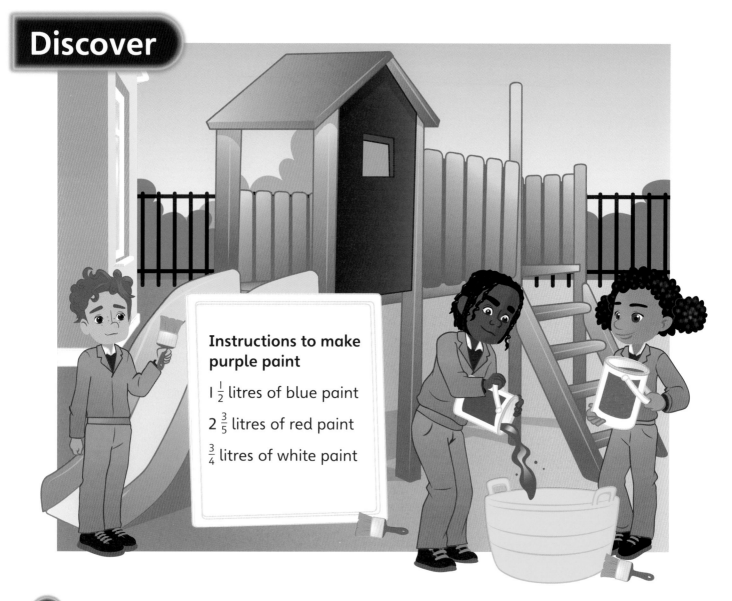

Instructions to make purple paint

$1\frac{1}{2}$ litres of blue paint

$2\frac{3}{5}$ litres of red paint

$\frac{3}{4}$ litres of white paint

❶ a) The children are going to make some purple paint using the instructions.

How many litres of purple paint will they make?

b) $3\frac{1}{2}$ litres of purple paint are needed to fully cover all the roofs.

$1\frac{1}{5}$ litres of purple paint are needed to paint the wooden poles.

Will there be enough paint to paint both the roofs and the poles?

Share

a)

Blue

Red

White

Method I

Add the red paint and blue paint: $2\frac{3}{5} + 1\frac{1}{2}$

Add the wholes: $2 + 1 = 3$

The lowest common denominator of 5 and 2 is 10.

Add the fractions: $\frac{3}{5} + \frac{1}{2} = \frac{6}{10} + \frac{5}{10} = \frac{11}{10} = 1\frac{1}{10}$

So $3 + 1\frac{1}{10} = 4\frac{1}{10}$

Now add on the white paint: $4\frac{1}{10} + \frac{3}{4} = 4\frac{2}{20} + \frac{15}{20} = 4\frac{17}{20}$

The total paint made is $4\frac{17}{20}$.

I added the red and blue paint first and then added the white paint.

Method 2

$2\frac{3}{5} + 1\frac{1}{2} + \frac{3}{4}$

Add the wholes: $2 + 1 + 0 = 3$

Add the parts: $\frac{3}{5} + \frac{1}{2} + \frac{3}{4} = \frac{12}{20} + \frac{10}{20} + \frac{15}{20}$

$$= \frac{37}{20}$$

$$= 1\frac{17}{20}$$

I added all the fractions at once.

Add the wholes and the parts: $3 + 1\frac{17}{20} = 4\frac{17}{20}$

The children will make $4\frac{17}{20}$ litres of purple paint.

b) Paint needed for the roofs and the poles: $3\frac{1}{2} + 1\frac{1}{5}$

Add the wholes: $3 + 1 = 4$

Add the parts: $\frac{1}{2} + \frac{1}{5} = \frac{5}{10} + \frac{2}{10} = \frac{7}{10}$

Add the wholes and the parts: $4 + \frac{7}{10} = 4\frac{7}{10}$

Compare the fractions using equivalent fractions with a common denominator.

$4\frac{7}{10} = 4\frac{14}{20}$

$4\frac{17}{20} > 4\frac{14}{20}$ so there will be enough purple paint to paint the roofs and the poles.

Think together

1 Holly makes a wedding cake.

Calculate the total height of the cake using the two different methods.

The total height of the cake is $\boxed{}\,\frac{\boxed{}}{\boxed{}}$ inches.

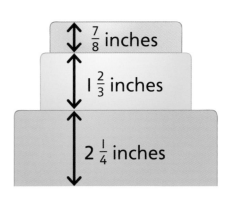

$\frac{7}{8}$ inches

$1\frac{2}{3}$ inches

$2\frac{1}{4}$ inches

2 Work out the missing numbers.

a) $\boxed{}\,\frac{\boxed{}}{\boxed{}} - 2\frac{1}{3} = 1\frac{5}{6}$

b) $2\frac{1}{3} - \frac{\boxed{}}{\boxed{}} = 1\frac{5}{6}$

3 Lee has some sheets of card.

Area = $15\frac{4}{9}$ cm²   Area = $17\frac{1}{6}$ cm²

Lee places the star on the blue card and sticks it down. What is the area of the blue background?

I think you need to add the areas together because you are putting them together.

I am not sure that is correct.

163

→ **Practice book 6A p117**

Problem solving – adding and subtracting fractions ②

Discover

Aki

Bella

1 **a)** Aki's bowling balls have a total mass of $15\frac{3}{4}$ kg.

Bella's bowling balls have a total mass of $11\frac{1}{12}$ kg.

Work out the mass of one yellow ball.

b) Work out the mass of one red striped ball.

Share

a)

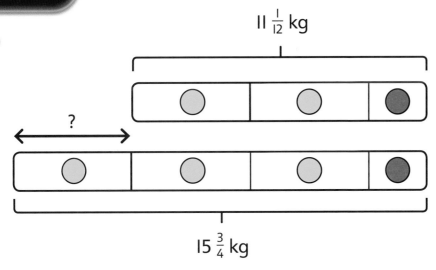

$11\frac{1}{12}$ kg

?

$15\frac{3}{4}$ kg

I drew a bar model. I worked out the mass of one yellow bowling ball by subtracting.

Mass of 1 yellow bowling ball $= 15\frac{3}{4} - 11\frac{1}{12}$

$15\frac{3}{4} = 15\frac{9}{12}$

$15\frac{9}{12} - 11\frac{1}{12} = 4\frac{8}{12}$ $4\frac{8}{12} = 4\frac{2}{3}$

The mass of 1 yellow bowling ball is $4\frac{2}{3}$ kg.

b)

| $4\frac{2}{3}$ | $4\frac{2}{3}$ | ⬤ |

$11\frac{1}{12}$ kg

Now I know the mass of each yellow bowling ball I can put this into my model.

The mass of 2 yellow bowling balls is

$4\frac{2}{3} + 4\frac{2}{3} = 8\frac{4}{3} = 8 + 1\frac{1}{3} = 9\frac{1}{3}$ kg

$11\frac{1}{12} = 10 + \frac{13}{12}$

So $10\frac{13}{12} - 9\frac{1}{3} = 10\frac{13}{12} - 9\frac{4}{12} = 1\frac{9}{12}$

$1\frac{9}{12} = 1\frac{3}{4}$

The mass of one red striped bowling ball is $1\frac{3}{4}$ kg.

Think together

1 What fraction of the shape is not shaded?

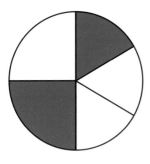

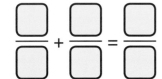 of the shape is not shaded.

2 Kate is cycling to the beach. It is $6\frac{1}{3}$ km from her house.

She cycles for $2\frac{4}{5}$ km, has a break and then cycles for another $1\frac{2}{3}$ km.

How much further does she need to cycle?

3 Three points are marked on a number line.

C is $1\frac{5}{6}$ less than B.

How much bigger is C than A?

4 Mo's house has a square shaped kitchen and a rectangle shaped living room.

Which room has the bigger perimeter?

How much bigger?

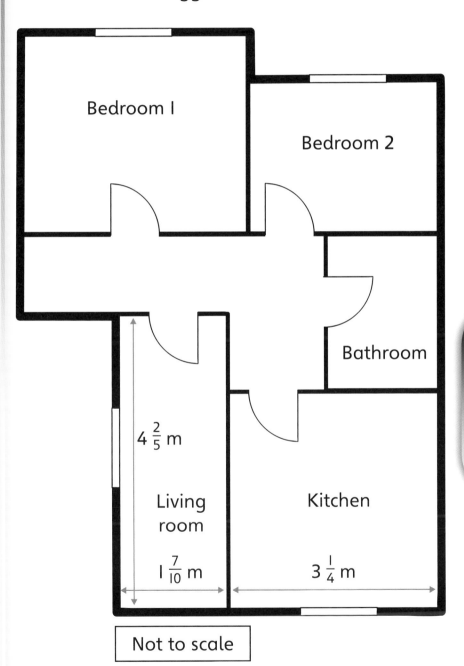

Bedroom 1

Bedroom 2

Bathroom

Living room

$4\frac{2}{5}$ m

$1\frac{7}{10}$ m

Kitchen

$3\frac{1}{4}$ m

Not to scale

I must think what I know about squares and rectangles. I wonder if I have to add all four sides together to work out the answers.

167

→ Practice book 6A p120

End of unit check

1 What is $\frac{2}{3} + \frac{3}{5}$?

A $1\frac{4}{15}$ **B** $1\frac{9}{15}$ **C** $\frac{5}{8}$ **D** $\frac{5}{15}$

2 How much does the pear weigh?

A $\frac{3}{8}$ kg   **B** $\frac{11}{40}$ kg   **C** $\frac{4}{18}$ kg   **D** $\frac{19}{40}$ kg

3 Which one of these fractions is the biggest?

A $\frac{3}{4}$ **B** $\frac{4}{5}$ **C** $\frac{3}{5}$ **D** $\frac{7}{10}$

4 What is $2\frac{1}{5} + 3\frac{5}{6}$?

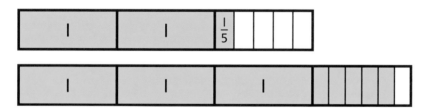

A $5\frac{6}{11}$ **B** $5\frac{6}{30}$ **C** $5\frac{1}{30}$ **D** $6\frac{1}{30}$

5 What is the missing denominator?

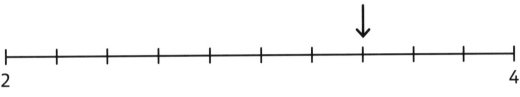

$$1\frac{1}{4} + 1\frac{1}{\boxed{}} = 2\frac{9}{12}$$

A 3   **B** 12   **C** 2   **D** 8

6 What is the number shown by the arrow?

2   4

A $2\frac{7}{10}$ **B** 2·7   **C** $3\frac{7}{10}$ **D** $3\frac{2}{5}$

7 At the school fete Lee is helping at the cake stall. He has $3\frac{1}{2}$ cakes.

Lee sells $2\frac{1}{6}$ cakes.

How many cakes does he have left?

169

→ Practice book 6A p123

Unit 5
Fractions ❷

In this unit we will …

- ⚡ Multiply any fraction by a whole number or another fraction
- ⚡ Divide a fraction by a whole number
- ⚡ Solve problems involving all four operations with fractions
- ⚡ Solve problems involving a fraction of an amount

You will be able to multiply a fraction by a fraction by showing each fraction on the side of a grid. What is $\frac{1}{2} \times \frac{3}{4}$?

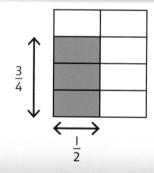

We will need some maths words.
How many of these can you remember?

numerator   **denominator**   **whole number**

mixed number   **proper fraction**

improper fraction   **convert**   **simplify**

We can use a fraction strip above a number line to help us multiply a fraction by a whole number and convert between improper fractions and mixed numbers. What is $\frac{2}{3} \times 4$ as a mixed number?

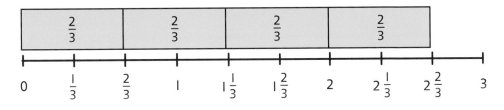

Multiplying a fraction by a whole number

Discover

1. **a)** The boat uses $\frac{1}{3}$ of a tank of fuel for each trip.

   How many tanks of fuel are used in a day?

   b) What is the total duration of the boat trips in a day?

Share

a) Each trip uses $\frac{1}{3}$ of a tank of fuel.

There are 5 trips in a day.

$\frac{1}{3} + \frac{1}{3} + \frac{1}{3} + \frac{1}{3} + \frac{1}{3} = \frac{5}{3} = 1\frac{2}{3}$

or

$\frac{1}{3} \times 5 = \frac{5}{3} = 1\frac{2}{3}$

$1\frac{2}{3}$ tanks of fuel are used in a day.

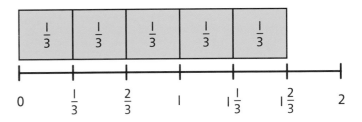

b) Each boat trip takes $1\frac{1}{4}$ hours and there are 5 trips a day.

I can multiply the whole and the fraction separately and then add them.

I will convert the mixed number to an improper fraction first.

Method 1

$1 \times 5 = 5$

$\frac{1}{4} \times 5 = \frac{5}{4} = 1\frac{1}{4}$

$5 + 1\frac{1}{4} = 6\frac{1}{4}$

Method 2

$1\frac{1}{4} = \frac{5}{4}$

$\frac{5}{4} \times 5 = \frac{25}{4}$

$\frac{25}{4} = 6\frac{1}{4}$

The total duration of the boat trips in a day is $6\frac{1}{4}$ hours.

Think together

1 On Saturday the boat makes 7 trips. It uses $\frac{1}{3}$ of a tank of fuel for each trip.

How many tanks of fuel are used on Saturday?

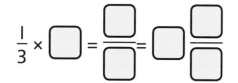

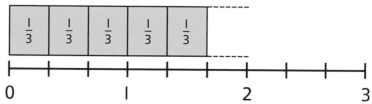

tanks of fuel are used.

2 A fishing boat offers fishing trips. During each trip the boat travels $1\frac{2}{5}$ km.

How far does the boat travel in 4 trips? Work out the answer using both methods.

Method 1

$$\boxed{} \times 4 = \boxed{}$$

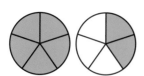 × 4 =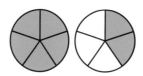

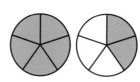 =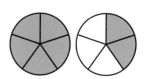

Method 2

The boat travels $\boxed{}\frac{\boxed{}}{\boxed{}}$ km.

174

CHALLENGE

3 **a)** Complete the multiplications.

$\frac{1}{4} \times 2 = \frac{2}{4}$

$\frac{1}{6} \times 5 = \frac{5}{6}$

$\frac{1}{4} \times 3 = \frac{3}{4}$

$\frac{2}{6} \times 5 = \frac{\square}{\square}$

$\frac{1}{4} \times 5 = \frac{\square}{\square}$

$\frac{5}{6} \times 5 = \frac{\square}{\square}$

$\frac{1}{4} \times 9 = \frac{\square}{\square}$

$1\frac{1}{6} \times 5 = \frac{\square}{\square}$

What patterns do you notice?

Can you find a quick way to get the answers?

I notice something between the numerator of the fraction, the whole number and the numerator of the final answer.

b) Find three fractions that multiply by a whole number to make these numbers.

$\frac{5}{8}$ $\qquad$ $\frac{10}{9}$ $\qquad$ $1\frac{1}{5}$

→ **Practice book 6A p126**

Multiplying a fraction by a fraction ①

Discover

① Bella and Amal are making flapjacks.

a) They have $\frac{1}{2}$ a bag of oats. They need to use $\frac{1}{2}$ of the oats in the bag.

What fraction of a whole bag do they need to use?

b) They have $\frac{3}{4}$ of a block of butter.

They need $\frac{1}{2}$ of this to make the flapjack.

What fraction of a whole block do they need to use?

Share

a) There is $\frac{1}{2}$ a bag of oats.

Bella and Amal need to use $\frac{1}{2}$ of the oats in the bag.

> I used a grid. I labelled $\frac{1}{2}$ along the bottom and $\frac{1}{2}$ on the side. I shaded in the part of the grid where the $\frac{1}{2}$ labels lined up.

  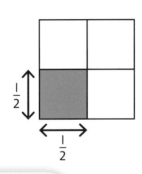

> I think $\frac{1}{2}$ of $\frac{1}{2}$ means the same as $\frac{1}{2} \times \frac{1}{2}$.

$\frac{1}{2}$ of $\frac{1}{2}$ is equal to $\frac{1}{4}$.

Write this as $\frac{1}{2} \times \frac{1}{2} = \frac{1}{4}$.

Bella and Amal need to use $\frac{1}{4}$ of a bag of oats.

b)

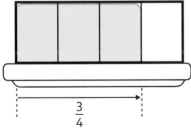 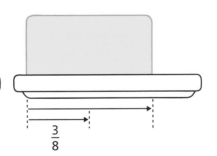 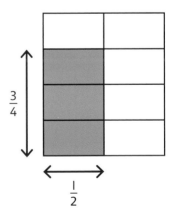

$\frac{1}{2}$ of $\frac{3}{4}$ is equal to $\frac{3}{8}$.

$\frac{1}{2} \times \frac{3}{4} = \frac{3}{8}$

Bella and Amal need to use $\frac{3}{8}$ of a block of butter.

177

Think together

1 Bella is now making brownies.

The bag of sugar is $\frac{1}{3}$ full. Bella uses $\frac{1}{3}$ of the sugar in the bag.

What fraction of the bag will she use?

  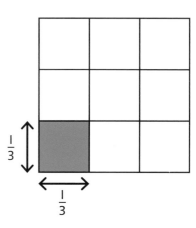

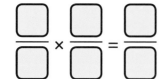 Bella will use ⬜/⬜ of the bag of sugar.

2 The brownies take $\frac{2}{3}$ of an hour to cook.

Amal is going to check on them when they have been cooking for $\frac{3}{4}$ of the time needed.

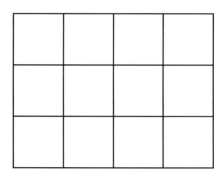

What fraction of the hour will have passed when Amal checks on the brownies?

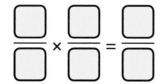

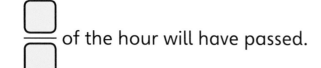 of the hour will have passed.

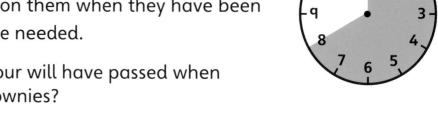

3 **a)** Amelia and Richard are working out $\frac{1}{4} \times \frac{2}{5}$.

Amelia

Richard

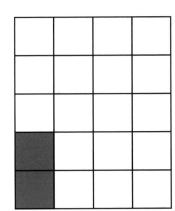

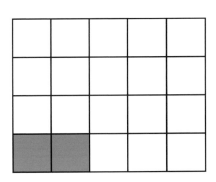

Which diagram is correct? Explain why.

Remember, you could also write this multiplication as $\frac{1}{4}$ of $\frac{2}{5}$.

b) Use diagrams to work out these calculations.

$\frac{1}{3} \times \frac{3}{4}$ $\frac{2}{5}$ of $\frac{1}{4}$

179

→ **Practice book 6A p129**

Multiplying a fraction by a fraction ②

Discover

1 **a)** Use diagrams to find the answers to the calculations.

b) Look at your answers.

How can you work out the answers without diagrams?

Share

a)

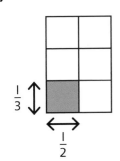 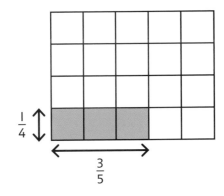 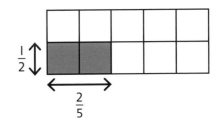

The total number of blocks gives the denominator of the answer.

The number of shaded blocks gives the numerator of the answer.

$$\frac{1}{2} \times \frac{1}{3} = \frac{1}{6}$$ $$\frac{3}{5} \times \frac{1}{4} = \frac{3}{20}$$ $$\frac{2}{5} \times \frac{1}{2} = \frac{2}{10}$$

> I noticed that I multiply the numerators together and the denominators together.

b) $\frac{1}{2} \times \frac{1}{3} = \frac{1 \times 1}{2 \times 3} = \frac{1}{6}$

$\frac{3}{5} \times \frac{1}{4} = \frac{3 \times 1}{5 \times 4} = \frac{3}{20}$

> I think I can simplify the last answer by dividing both the numerator and the denominator by 2.

$\frac{2}{5} \times \frac{1}{2} = \frac{2 \times 1}{5 \times 2} = \frac{2}{10}$

So $\frac{2}{5} \times \frac{1}{2} = \frac{1}{5}$.

Think together

1 **a)** Use a diagram to work out $\frac{2}{3} \times \frac{4}{5}$.

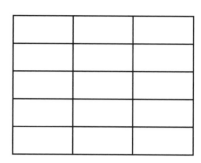

$$\frac{2}{3} \times \frac{4}{5} = \frac{\Box}{\Box}$$

b) Now find the answer by multiplying the numerators and the denominators.

$$\frac{2}{3} \times \frac{4}{5} = \frac{\Box \times \Box}{\Box \times \Box} = \frac{\Box}{\Box}$$

Check your answer is the same.

2 Work out these calculations. Give each answer in its simplest form.

a) $\frac{3}{7} \times \frac{5}{6} = \frac{\Box \times \Box}{\Box \times \Box} = \frac{\Box}{\Box} = \frac{\Box}{\Box}$

b) $\frac{9}{10} \times \frac{2}{17} = \frac{\Box \times \Box}{\Box \times \Box} = \frac{\Box}{\Box} = \frac{\Box}{\Box}$

c) $\frac{2}{3} \times \frac{1}{4} \times \frac{1}{2} = \frac{\Box}{\Box}$

Why would drawing a diagram not be efficient for part b)?

3 **a)** Two fractions have been multiplied together.

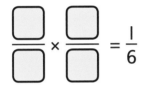

$$\frac{\square}{\square} \times \frac{\square}{\square} = \frac{5}{9}$$

What could the fractions be?

How many different answers can you find?

b) Two more fractions have been multiplied together.

$$\frac{\square}{\square} \times \frac{\square}{\square} = \frac{1}{6}$$

One of the fractions is $\frac{2}{3}$.

What is the other fraction?

Is there more than one answer?

I do not think this works. Both numerators would have to be 1.

I wonder if the answer was simplified.

183

Dividing a fraction by a whole number

Discover

Make a pop-up card

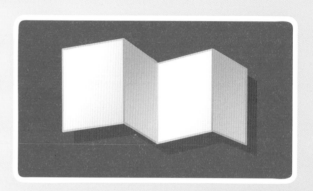

For the spring
- Fold a paper strip into quarters.
- Divide one of the quarters at the end of the strip into 2.
- Put glue on one of these 2 parts at the end of the strip.

Instructions

For the penguin's body
- Divide a circle into thirds.
- Divide one of the thirds into 2 equal parts.
- Leave one of these 2 parts white and put it at the top. Colour the rest of the circle black.

 a) What fraction of the penguin's body is white?

b) What fraction of the strip of paper is covered in glue?

Share

a) The circle is divided into thirds.

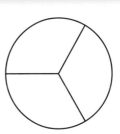

One of the thirds is divided into 2 equal parts.

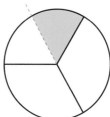

There are 6 of these equal parts in the circle.

$\frac{1}{3} \div 2 = \frac{1}{6}$

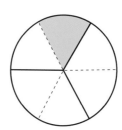

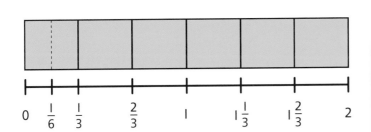

$\frac{1}{6}$ of the penguin's body is white.

I divide $\frac{1}{3}$ into 2. This is the same as dividing $\frac{1}{3}$ by 2. When I divide $\frac{1}{3}$ by 2, I can see that I have $\frac{1}{6}$.

b) The strip of paper is folded into quarters.

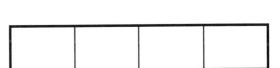

One of the quarters is divided into 2.

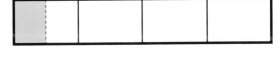

There are 8 equal parts this size.

$\frac{1}{4} \div 2 = \frac{1}{8}$

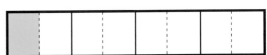

$\frac{1}{8}$ of the strip of paper is covered in glue.

Think together

1 Divide a circle into quarters.

Divide 1 of the quarters into 3 parts. Shade in 1 of these parts.

What fraction of the circle is shaded?

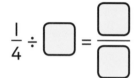

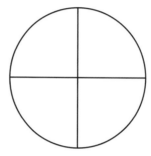 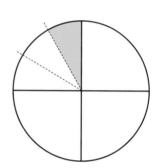

$\dfrac{\Box}{\Box}$ of the circle is shaded.

2 Fold a strip of paper into thirds.

Divide 1 of the thirds into 3 parts. Shade in 1 of these parts.

What fraction of the paper is shaded?

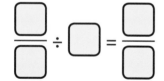

$\dfrac{\Box}{\Box}$ of the paper is shaded.

3 **a)** Here are the calculations you have done so far.

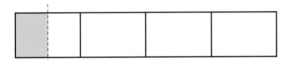

$\frac{1}{3} \div 2 = \frac{1}{6}$

$\frac{1}{4} \div 3 = \frac{1}{12}$

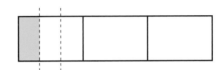

$\frac{1}{4} \div 2 = \frac{1}{8}$

$\frac{1}{3} \div 3 = \frac{1}{9}$

What is the same about each calculation?

What is different?

b) What do you notice about the answers?

Is there a way you can find the answer without drawing the diagram?

Use your method to work out these divisions.

$\frac{1}{6} \div 2 = \dfrac{\Box}{\Box}$ $\frac{1}{4} \div 4 = \dfrac{\Box}{\Box}$ $\frac{1}{5} \div 3 = \dfrac{\Box}{\Box}$

Check your answers using diagrams.

I think I can see a method for finding the denominator of the fraction in the answer.

187

Dividing a fraction by a whole number ❷

Discover

I have $\frac{4}{5}$ of the jug of juice left.

1 **a)** The jug is $\frac{4}{5}$ full of juice.

The juice is divided equally between the 2 empty cups.

What fraction of the original jug is in each of these cups?

b) $\frac{9}{10}$ of the jar of baby food will be enough for 3 equal meals.

What fraction of the jar of baby food should be put into each bowl?

Share

a) There is $\frac{4}{5}$ of the jug to be shared equally between 2 cups.

I drew a diagram to represent the juice in the jug and then I divided this by 2. I can write this as a division.

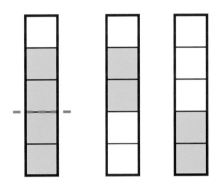

$$\frac{4}{5} \div 2 = \frac{2}{5}$$

$\frac{2}{5}$ of the original jug is in each cup.

b) There is $\frac{9}{10}$ of the jar to be shared equally into 3 bowls.

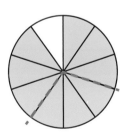 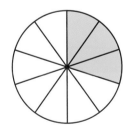 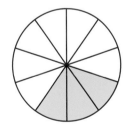 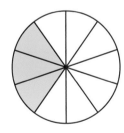

     jar   bowl 1   bowl 2   bowl 3

$$\frac{9}{10} \div 3 = \frac{3}{10}$$

$\frac{3}{10}$ of the jar of baby food should be put into each bowl.

Think together

1 A packet of rusks is $\frac{6}{7}$ full.

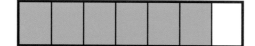

Draw a diagram to show how the biscuits can be shared equally between the 3 babies.

Write this as a division calculation.

$$\frac{6}{7} \div 3 = \frac{\boxed{}}{\boxed{}}$$

What fraction of the packet does each baby get?

Each baby gets $\dfrac{\boxed{}}{\boxed{}}$ of the packet.

2 What division calculations are shown?

a)

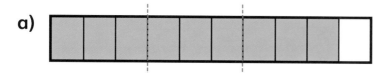

$$\frac{\boxed{}}{\boxed{}} \div \boxed{} = \frac{\boxed{}}{\boxed{}}$$

b)

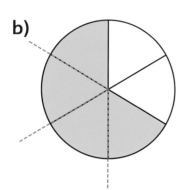

$$\frac{\boxed{}}{\boxed{}} \div \boxed{} = \frac{\boxed{}}{\boxed{}}$$

3 **a)** Use the diagrams to complete these calculations.

CHALLENGE

$\frac{3}{5} \div 3 = \dfrac{\square}{\square}$

$\dfrac{\square}{\square} \div 4 = \dfrac{\square}{\square}$

> I think there is a link between the numerators and what I am dividing by. I will check whether this works with the other questions I have done.

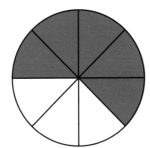

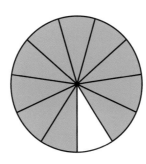

$\dfrac{\square}{\square} \div 5 = \dfrac{\square}{\square}$

$\dfrac{\square}{\square} \div 5 = \dfrac{\square}{\square}$

Is there a way you can find each answer without drawing a diagram?

b) Work out the missing fractions without using a diagram.

$\frac{3}{4} \div 3 = \dfrac{\square}{\square}$

$\frac{12}{25} \div 3 = \dfrac{\square}{\square}$

> I will check my answers using diagrams.

$\frac{8}{9} \div 2 = \dfrac{\square}{\square}$

$\dfrac{\square}{\square} \div 4 = \frac{2}{9}$

191

→ **Practice book 6A p138**

Dividing a fraction by a whole number **3**

Discover

I **a)** The bamboo shoots are $\frac{2}{3}$ m long.

If the pandas share one bamboo shoot equally, how much will each panda get?

b) Another panda comes along to share the bamboo shoot.

How much will each panda get now?

Share

a) The bamboo shoot is $\frac{2}{3}$ m long.

3 pandas share the shoot equally.

> I drew a bar model. I shaded in $\frac{2}{3}$. I do not think I can share this equally between 3 pandas, can I?

> Yes, you can. I divided each $\frac{1}{3}$ into 3 so I could give each panda a part of the bamboo. This is the same as $\frac{6}{9}$ m divided by 3.

I m

bamboo shoot

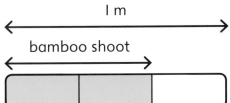

I m

bamboo shoot

$\frac{2}{3} \div 3 = \frac{6}{9} \div 3$

$\frac{6}{9} \div 3 = \frac{2}{9}$

Each panda will get $\frac{2}{9}$ m of bamboo shoot.

b) There are now 4 pandas.

$$\frac{2}{3} \div 4 = \frac{8}{12} \div 4$$

$$= \frac{2}{12}$$

$$= \frac{1}{6}$$

Each panda will get $\frac{1}{6}$ m of bamboo shoot.

I wonder if I need to divide each part into 4. I did it by dividing each part into 2.

Think together

1 A bamboo shoot is $\frac{5}{6}$ metre long. Share this between 3 pandas.

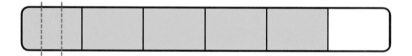

$$\frac{5}{6} \div 3 = \frac{\boxed{}}{\boxed{}} \div 3 = \frac{\boxed{}}{\boxed{}}$$

Each panda will get $\frac{\boxed{}}{\boxed{}}$ m of bamboo shoot.

194

2 Use the diagram to help you work out $\frac{3}{5} \div 6$.

$$\frac{3}{5} \div 6 = \frac{\square}{\square}$$

3 **a)** Max and Ambika are working out $\frac{2}{3} \div 6$.

 CHALLENGE

I will divide each $\frac{1}{3}$ into 6 pieces.

Max

I will divide each $\frac{1}{3}$ into 3 pieces.

Ambika

Will they get the same answer? Show all the calculations.

Whose method do you prefer?

b) Use Max and Ambika's methods to work out $\frac{3}{4} \div 6$.

I drew a diagram to represent $\frac{3}{4}$ and then divided each part into 6 equal pieces.

I do not think you needed to do that. Look at the pattern between the numerator and the number we are dividing by.

→ Practice book 6A p141

Four rules with fractions

Discover

I **a)** How far did Luis walk from Monday to Friday?

b) Luis's target was to walk 5 km in total in the week.

Did he meet his target?

Share

a) Luis walked $\frac{2}{3}$ km each day from Monday to Friday.

?

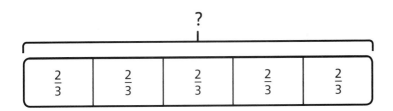

$\frac{2}{3} + \frac{2}{3} + \frac{2}{3} + \frac{2}{3} + \frac{2}{3} = \frac{10}{3} = 3\frac{1}{3}$ or $\frac{2}{3} \times 5 = \frac{10}{3} = 3\frac{1}{3}$

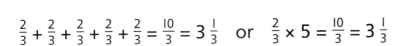

I could add or multiply to work out the answer.

Luis walked $3\frac{1}{3}$ km from Monday to Friday.

b) Luis's goal was to walk 5 km in total in the week.

He walked $\frac{7}{9}$ km on Saturday and $\frac{7}{9}$ km on Sunday.

$\frac{2}{3} \times 5 = \frac{10}{3}$ $\frac{7}{9} \times 2 = \frac{14}{9}$

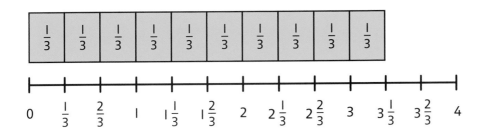

I worked out Monday to Friday first and then the weekend. I added the answers by finding a common denominator.

$\frac{10}{3} + \frac{14}{9} = \frac{30}{9} + \frac{14}{9} = \frac{44}{9} = 4\frac{8}{9}$

$4\frac{8}{9} < 5$, so Luis did not meet his target.

Think together

1 Max is working out the perimeter of this rectangle.

 $\frac{1}{6}$ m

$\frac{3}{4}$ m

I multiplied the length by 2 and the width by 2 and then added together.

Max

Work out the perimeter using Max's method.

$\frac{3}{4} \times 2 = \dfrac{\Box}{\Box}$ $\frac{1}{6} \times 2 = \dfrac{\Box}{\Box}$

$\dfrac{\Box}{\Box} + \dfrac{\Box}{\Box} = \dfrac{\Box}{\Box} + \dfrac{\Box}{\Box}$

$= \dfrac{\Box}{\Box} = \dfrac{\Box}{\Box}$

$= \Box \dfrac{\Box}{\Box}$

The perimeter of the rectangle is $\Box \dfrac{\Box}{\Box}$ m.

2 What is the area of the shaded part of the rectangle?

$\frac{1}{2} \times \dfrac{\Box}{\Box} \times \dfrac{\Box}{\Box} = \dfrac{\Box}{\Box}$

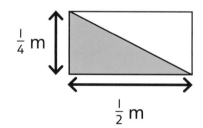

$\frac{1}{4}$ m

$\frac{1}{2}$ m

The area of the shaded part is $\dfrac{\Box}{\Box}$ m².

3 Jamilla and Alex have worked out the answer to this calculation.

$$\frac{1}{5} + \frac{3}{5} \times \frac{1}{4}$$

I think the answer is $\frac{7}{20}$.

I think the answer is $\frac{1}{5}$.

Jamilla

Alex

a) Whose answer is correct?

b) Explain how Jamilla and Alex worked out their answers. Explain why one of them is wrong.

You need to remember the order of operations. Which operation do you do first – multiplication or addition?

199

Calculating fractions of amounts

Discover

200 apples

Year 6　Year 6　Year 5　Year 4　Year 3

1 a) The apples are shared into the baskets equally.

How many apples will the Year 6 children get?

b) The Year 6 children eat $\frac{3}{10}$ of their apples in the morning and the remaining apples in the afternoon.

How many apples do they eat in the afternoon?

Share

a) There are 200 apples in the box.

The apples are shared equally between the baskets.

> There are only 4 year groups, so will Year 6 receive $\frac{1}{4}$ of the apples, which is 50?

> No, there are two baskets for Year 6, so the apples are shared between 5 baskets.

200 apples

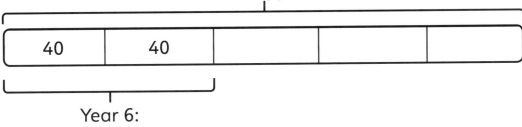

Year 6:
80 apples

The 200 apples are shared between 5 baskets.

$\frac{1}{5}$ of 200 = 200 ÷ 5 = 40

There are 2 baskets for Year 6. The Year 6 children will get $\frac{2}{5}$ of the apples.

$\frac{2}{5}$ of 200 = 2 × 40 = 80

The Year 6 children will get **80** apples.

b) The Year 6 children eat $\frac{3}{10}$ of their apples in the morning.

$\frac{1}{10}$ of 80 = 8

$\frac{3}{10}$ of 80 = 3 × 8 = 24

80 − 24 = 56

The Year 6 children eat 56 apples in the afternoon.

80 apples

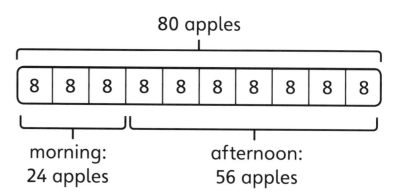

morning: 24 apples

afternoon: 56 apples

I just found $\frac{7}{10}$ of 80. If the children eat $\frac{3}{10}$ in the morning, they eat $\frac{7}{10}$ in the afternoon.

Think together

1 $\frac{5}{6}$ of this bag of flour is needed for a cake. How much flour is needed for the cake?

300 g

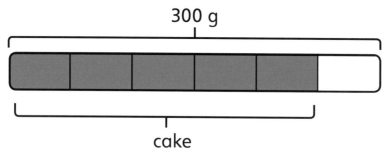

cake

$\frac{1}{6}$ of 300 g is 300 ÷ ☐ = ☐ g

$\frac{5}{6}$ of 300 g is ☐ × ☐ = ☐ g

☐ g of flour is needed.

2 There are 28 children in a Year 6 class. $\frac{5}{7}$ of the children are going on a school trip.

How many children are **not** going on the trip?

☐ children are not going on the trip.

> I think I could complete this question without subtracting.

3 There are 36 children in a swimming lesson.

CHALLENGE

$\frac{1}{3}$ of the children are boys. $\frac{1}{2}$ of the boys wear goggles.

Mo and Richard are working out how many of the boys wear goggles.

> I think 18 boys wear goggles, because $\frac{1}{2}$ of 36 is 18.

Mo

> I did 36 ÷ 3 = 12. I think 12 of the boys wear goggles.

 Richard

Mo and Richard are both incorrect.

What mistakes have they made?

What is the correct answer?

> Remember, you can draw a bar model to help you.

→ **Practice book 6A p147**

Problem solving – fractions of amounts

Discover

1 **a)** Lee spends $\frac{1}{4}$ of his pocket money on sweets.

How much pocket money did Lee have to begin with?

b) The jar was full before Lee bought any sweets.

Lee bought $\frac{2}{5}$ of the jar.

How many sweets were in the jar when it was full?

Share

a) Lee spends $\frac{1}{4}$ of his pocket money on sweets. The sweets cost £1·60.

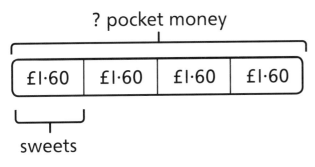

? pocket money

| £1·60 | £1·60 | £1·60 | £1·60 |

sweets

> When I first tried this, I made the mistake of finding $\frac{1}{4}$ of £1·60 to get £0·40. It is okay to make mistakes if I learn from them.

$\frac{1}{4}$ of his pocket money is £1·60.

£1·60 × 4 = £6·40

Lee had £6·40 to begin with.

b) The jar was full before Lee bought any sweets.

Lee bought $\frac{2}{5}$ of the jar.

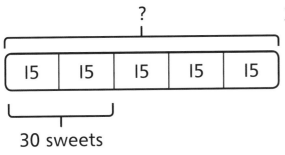

?

| 15 | 15 | 15 | 15 | 15 |

30 sweets

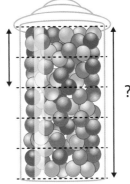

30 sweets

?

$\frac{2}{5}$ of the jar = 30 sweets

30 ÷ 2 = 15 sweets

15 sweets = $\frac{1}{5}$ of the jar

15 × 5 = 75

There were 75 sweets in the jar when it was full.

> To work it out I did 30 + 30 + 15 = 75 sweets.

Think together

1 Kate gets 24 darts.

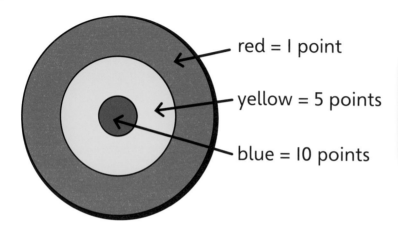

red = 1 point

yellow = 5 points

blue = 10 points

First, I am going to work out how many shots went in each section. I know how much each section is worth.

$\frac{1}{3}$ of Kate's darts go in the red section.

$\frac{1}{4}$ of them go in the yellow section.

The rest go in the blue section.

How many points does Kate score?

2 There are two pieces of rope.

$\frac{2}{3}$ of rope A is 3·6 m.

3·6 m

$\frac{1}{4}$ of rope B is 1·3 m.

1·3 m

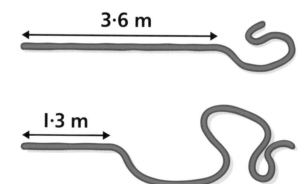

Which piece of rope is longer? By how much?

Rope _____ is longer by ⬚ m.

3 Amelia is thinking of a number.

$\frac{2}{3}$ of my number is 30.

What is $\frac{8}{9}$ of Amelia's number?

Remember, you can draw a bar model to help you.

I think I can work this out without having to find the original number. I can use my knowledge of equivalent fractions to help me.

Create similar questions of your own to ask a partner.

207

End of unit check

1 Work out $\frac{1}{3} \times \frac{2}{5}$.

   A $\frac{2}{15}$ **B** $\frac{3}{15}$ **C** $\frac{3}{8}$ **D** $\frac{2}{8}$

2 What is $\frac{1}{4} \div 2$?

   A 2 **B** $\frac{1}{2}$ **C** $\frac{1}{8}$ **D** $\frac{2}{4}$

3 Lee uses $\frac{5}{8}$ of a tin of tuna each day to make a sandwich.

How many tins of tuna will he need to make a sandwich every day for 4 days?

Give your answer in its simplest form.

   A $2\frac{2}{4}$ **B** $\frac{20}{32}$ **C** $2\frac{1}{2}$ **D** $\frac{5}{32}$

4 There are 30 children in a class. $\frac{2}{5}$ of the children are girls.
How many boys are in the class?

   A 12   **B** 18   **C** 30   **D** 75

5 $\frac{2}{3}$ of a number is 24. What is the number?

   A 8   **B** 16   **C** 24   **D** 36

6 What is the missing fraction?

$$\frac{2}{7} \div 4 = \frac{\boxed{}}{\boxed{}}$$

A $\frac{2}{7}$ **B** $\frac{8}{7}$ **C** $\frac{1}{14}$ **D** $1\frac{1}{14}$

7 How many hours are there in $\frac{3}{8}$ of a day?

A 24   **B** 9   **C** 8   **D** 3

8 Find the area of the rectangle.

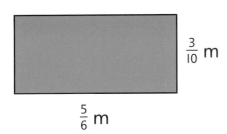

$\frac{3}{10}$ m

$\frac{5}{6}$ m

Give your answer in its simplest form.

9 $\frac{5}{9}$ of the pencils in a box are red.

There are 40 red pencils in the box.

How many pencils are in the box?

209

→ Practice book 6A p153

Unit 6
Geometry – position and direction

In this unit we will …

⚡ Look at how we can use coordinates to describe the position of a point on a grid

⚡ Look at how coordinates can have positive or negative values

⚡ Explore how we can use our knowledge of properties of shape to help us solve problems on a coordinate grid

⚡ Explore how we can move and change shapes on a coordinate grid, through translations and reflections

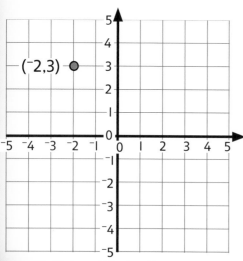

We are going to use grids like this in this unit. How is it different to what you have met before?

We will need some maths words.
Which ones have you seen before?

quadrant   four quadrants   translate

translation   *x*-axis   *y*-axis   axis

axes   horizontal   vertical

vertex   reflect   reflection

We will need this too! Can you work
out how we could describe the
position of the point on the grid?

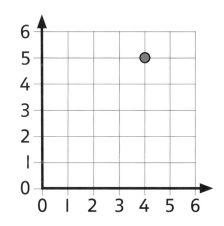

Plotting coordinates in the first quadrant

Discover

This grid represents the garden. A is the garden gnome, B is the shed and C is the slide. You will find the treasure at the missing vertex of this square, D. Where is it?

1 **a)** The points A, B and C are vertices of a square. The treasure is at the missing vertex, point D.

What coordinates take you to the treasure?

b) What is the perimeter of the square?

Share

a) B(8,7) is 3 metres away from A(5,7).

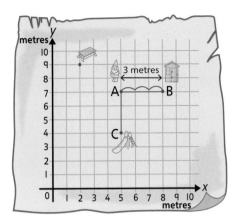

> The horizontal axis is called the *x*-axis. The vertical axis is called the *y*-axis. The *x*-axis is always given first in a set of coordinates.

> I will count how many metres point B is from point A. The missing point will be the same distance from B but downwards.

Counting 3 metres down from B(8,7) takes you to (8,4).
So D is (8,4), which is where the treasure is hidden.

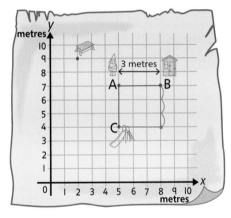

> I could count across from C.

b) The length of each side is 3 metres.
Therefore the perimeter is 3 × 4 = 12 metres.

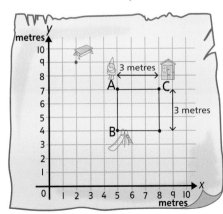

213

Think together

1 **a)** Find the missing vertex of this rectangle.

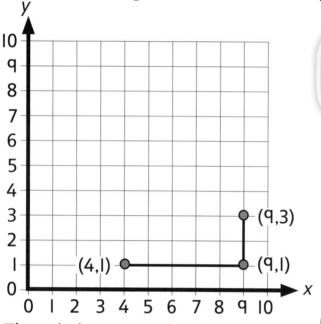

I could count up from one vertex or across from another to find the missing vertex.

The missing vertex is at coordinates (☐, ☐).

b) This line is part of a square.

What could two other vertices of the square be?

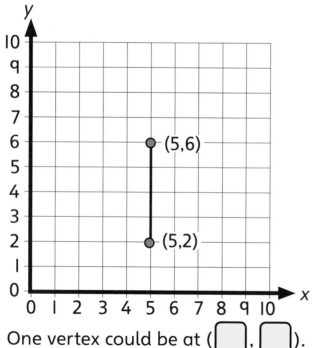

I think there is more than one correct solution.

One vertex could be at (☐, ☐).

Another vertex could be at (☐, ☐).

2 Point A of a rectangle is at (3, 4).
Work out the missing coordinates.

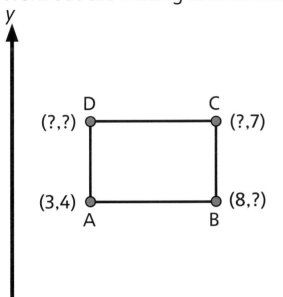

B (8, ☐)

C (☐, 7)

D (☐, ☐)

3 There are two identical isosceles triangles.
What are the coordinates of vertices A and B?

CHALLENGE

Vertex A (☐, ☐)

Vertex B (☐, ☐)

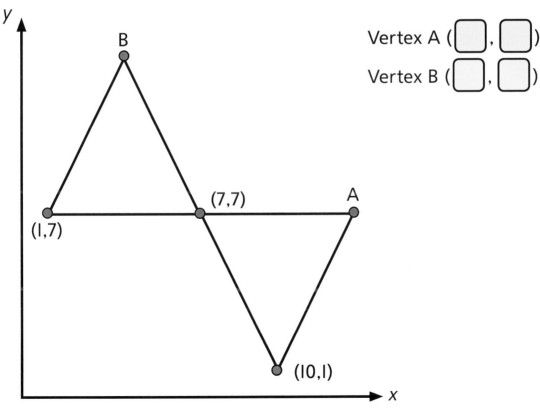

→ Practice book 6A p155

Plotting coordinates

Discover

1 a) What are the coordinates of the ships A and B?

b) Ambika guesses that Reena has a ship at the coordinates (⁻2,3).

Where is this point on the grid?

Share

a)

I think coordinates can also have negative values.

I remember that I should read the x-axis coordinate first, and then the y-axis coordinate.

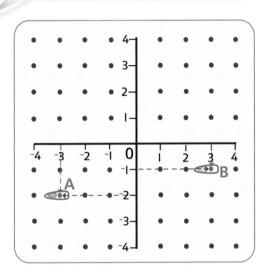

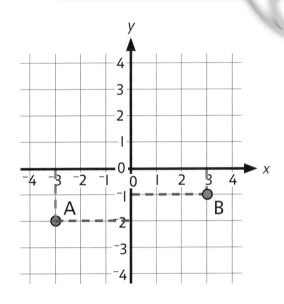

Ship A is in line with ⁻3 on the x-axis and it is in line with ⁻2 on the y-axis. The coordinates of ship A are (⁻3,⁻2).

Ship B is in line with 3 on the x-axis and it is in line with ⁻1 on the y-axis. The coordinates of ship B are (3,⁻1).

b)

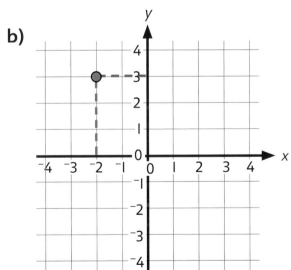

We say a coordinate grid like this has four **quadrants**. Coordinate grids that show just positive values have only one quadrant.

Point (⁻2,3) is at ⁻2 on the x-axis and 3 on the y-axis.

217

Think together

1 **a)** At what coordinates has Liam plotted his ships?

Ship A is at ⬜ on the *x*-axis and

it is at ⬜ on the *y*-axis.

The coordinates of ship A are

(⬜ , ⬜).

The coordinates of the other ships are:

Ship B (⬜ , ⬜)

Ship C (⬜ , ⬜)

Ship D (⬜ , ⬜)

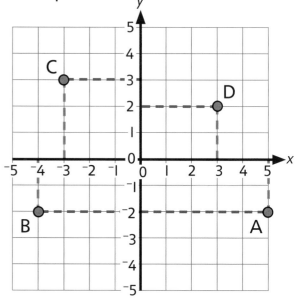

b) Liam guesses where his partner's ships are.

Guess 1 (⁻4,5)

Guess 2 (4,⁻2)

Guess 3 (⁻5,⁻4)

Point to each of his guesses
on the grid.

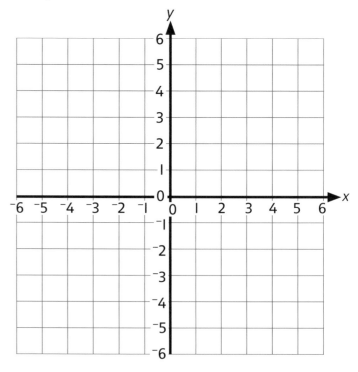

2 Mark says that his points are at:

A(1,⁻4)

B(2,3)

C(⁻5,⁻3)

D(⁻2,0)

Three of his coordinates are wrong. Can you work out which ones?

What mistakes did Mark make?

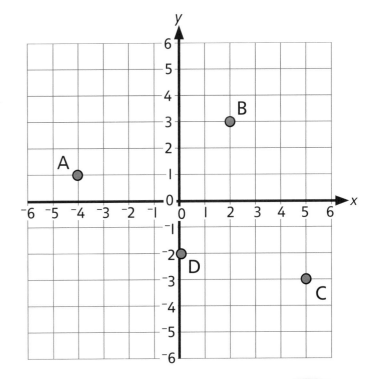

3 Maisy knows her partner's four points make a rectangle.

CHALLENGE

Which of the coordinates below are the coordinates of Maisy's partner's points?

(2,1)   (1,⁻1)   (2,⁻1)

(1,1)   (3,⁻2)   (2,⁻3)

(⁻1,1)   (⁻1,2)   (4,1)

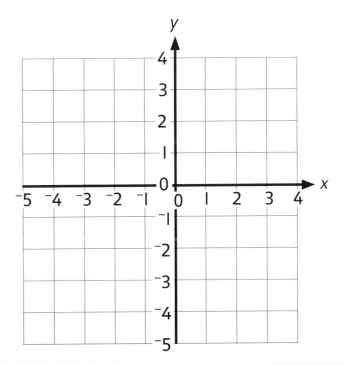

Plotting translations and reflections

Discover

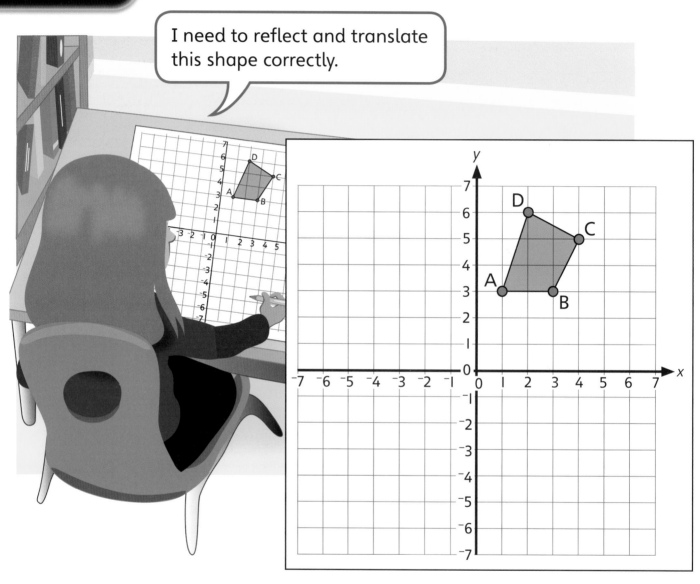

I need to reflect and translate this shape correctly.

1 **a)** Where would Olivia draw the shape if it was reflected in the *x*-axis?

b) Where would Olivia draw the shape if her original shape was translated 4 left and 5 down?

Share

You might find it useful to use tracing paper for reflections and translations.

I think when we **reflect** a shape, the new points will be the same distance away from the axis as the original points, just on the other side.

a) Reflect each point one at a time.

Points A and B are both 3 units away from the x-axis. Point C is 5 units away from the x-axis. Point D is 6 units away from the x-axis.

The reflected points will be the same distance away from the x-axis.

Join up the points in order to make the shape after it has been reflected.

The new coordinates are:
E is at (1,⁻3)
F is at (3,⁻3)
G is at (4,⁻5)
H is at (2,⁻6)

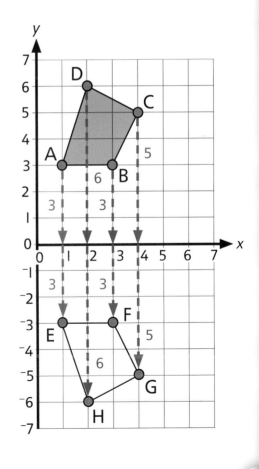

Translate means you move the vertices of the shape according to the instructions you are given.

I am going to move each point one at a time, and then join the points to make my shape.

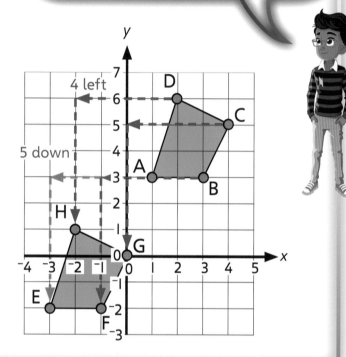

b) Start by moving point A. Move it 4 left first and then 5 down. Do the same with the other points.

Join up the points in order to make the new shape.

The new coordinates are:

E is at (⁻3,⁻2)

F is at (⁻1,⁻2)

G is at (0,0)

H is at (⁻2,1)

Think together

I **a)** Reflect shape A in the x-axis. Label your new shape B.

b) Reflect shape A in the y-axis. Label your new shape C.

To reflect in the y-axis, I think I need to work out the distance from the y-axis.

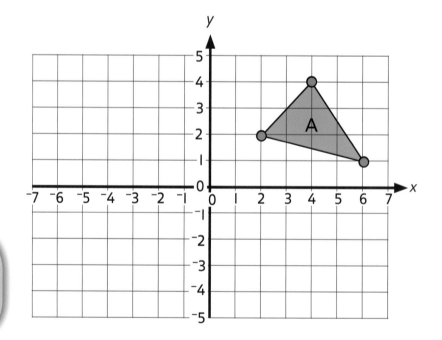

2 **a)** Translate shape D 2 units right and 3 units up. Label your new shape E.

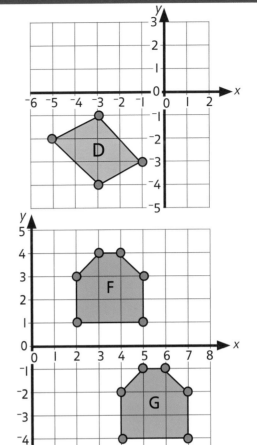

b) Look at this diagram. Complete the sentence:

Shape F has been translated

☐ ____ and ☐ ____ to

become shape G.

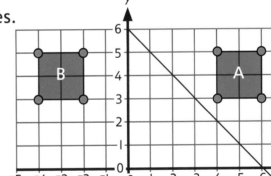

3 Spot and explain the mistakes.

a) Shape B should be a reflection of shape A in the diagonal line.

Explain what mistake has been made. Where should shape B be?

b) Shape D should be a translation of shape C, 4 units right and 3 units down.

Explain what mistake has been made. Where should shape D be?

CHALLENGE

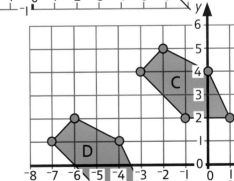

223

→ **Practice book 6A p161**

Reasoning about shapes with coordinates

Discover

The challenge is to move the robot to the different vertices of the shapes. Here are some clues to help you. Shape P is a square. Shape Q is identical to shape P.

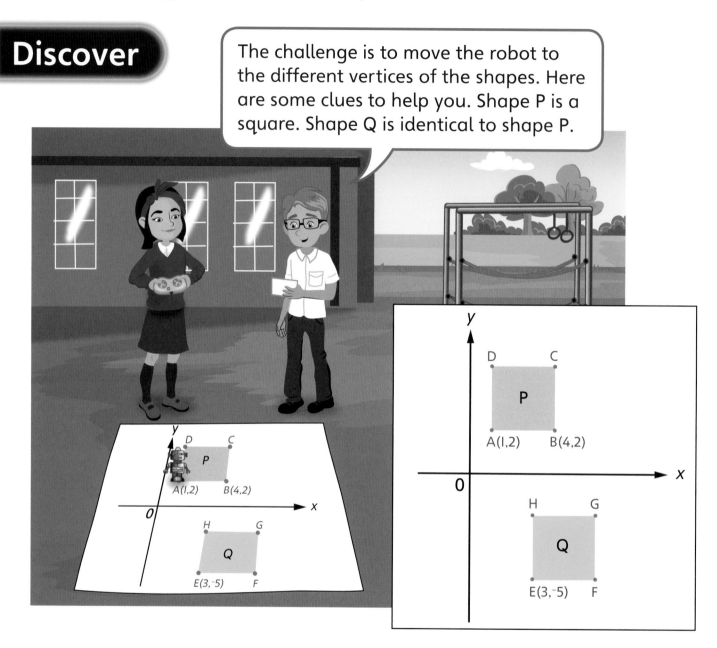

1 Lexi and Andy are trying to solve a puzzle.
They have been given some clues.

a) What are the coordinates of points C and D in shape P?

b) What are the coordinates of points F, G and H in shape Q?

Share

a) The line AB is 3 units long. This means the square has sides 3 units long.

D has the same *x*-coordinate as A but is 3 units higher on the *y*-axis than A. So the coordinates of vertex D are (1,5).

C has the same *x*-coordinate as B and the same *y*-coordinate as D. So the coordinates of vertex C are (4,5).

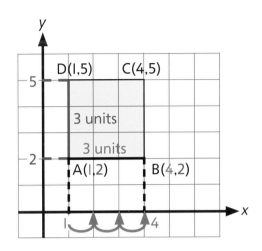

b) Shape Q is identical to shape P.

> I think I need to work out what the shape has been translated by first.
> I can do this by looking at the difference between vertex A and vertex E.

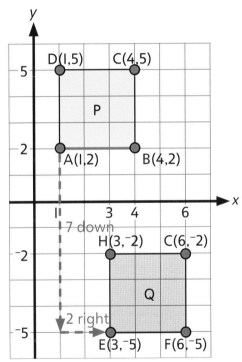

We know that vertex E is (3,⁻5). Vertex A has therefore been translated 2 units right and 7 units down.

So each vertex has been translated 2 units right and 7 units down.

The missing coordinates for shape Q are:

F (6,⁻5) G (6,⁻2) H (3,⁻2)

Think together

1 Eden and Noah have been given some axes showing two squares. The squares are identical.

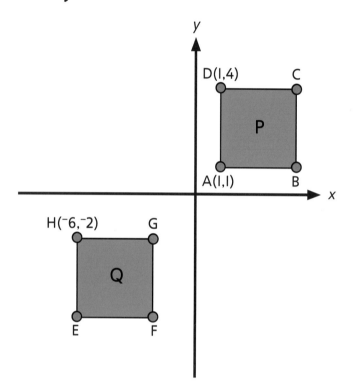

I will work out how many units long each side of the square is to help me.

a) What are the coordinates of points B and C?

Point B (☐ , ☐)

Point C (☐ , ☐)

b) What are the coordinates of points E, F and G?

Point E (☐ , ☐)

Point F (☐ , ☐)

Point G (☐ , ☐)

2 This is an isosceles triangle.

a) What are the coordinates of point C?

b) The triangle is translated. Point A has moved to where point D is. What are the coordinates of the other two vertices of the triangle?

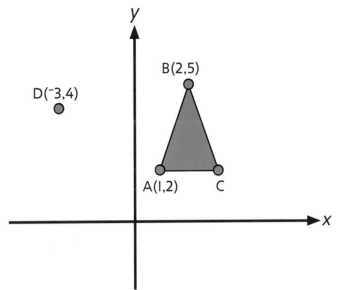

3 Eden and Noah have another puzzle to solve.

The triangles are identical.

What are the coordinates of vertices C, D and E?

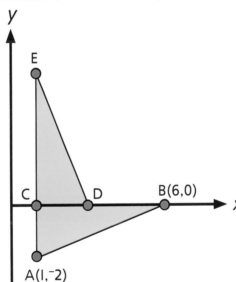

One side of the triangles is the same as the x-axis. I know this means it must be at 0 on the y-axis.

I can use the information I have to work out the length of two of the sides of the triangle.

227

End of unit check

1 What are the coordinates of point A?

A (2,⁻4)

B (⁻2,⁻4)

C (2,4)

D (⁻4,2)

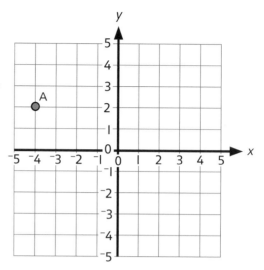

2 Points B and C are 2 vertices of a square. Which of the coordinates below could **not** be coordinates of another vertex of the same square?

A (5,⁻5)

B (5,1)

C (2,2)

D (2,1)

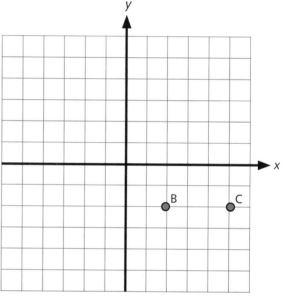

3 Which shape shows shape E after it has been reflected in the y-axis?

A Shape A

B Shape B

C Shape C

D Shape D

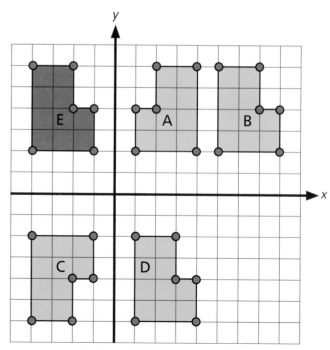

4 Shape A is translated and the result is Shape B. What was the translation?

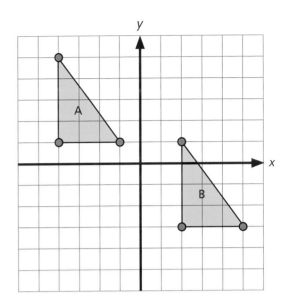

A Translation 6 left and 4 up

B Translation 4 right and 4 down

C Translation 6 right and 4 down

D Translation 6 right and 5 down

Think carefully about how you can use the information you have.

5 The diagram shows two identical rectangles.

Find the coordinates of point D.

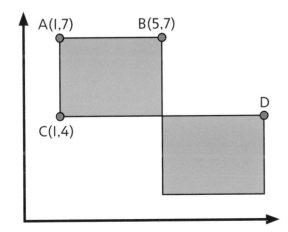

229

→ Practice book 6A p167

I did not give up, even when I found some things difficult.

It was fun finding different ways to solve problems.

What have we learnt?

Can you do all these things?

⚡ Solve problems involving numbers up to 10,000,000

⚡ Compare and order numbers up to 10,000,000

⚡ Multiply and divide numbers up to 4 digits by a 1 digit number

⚡ Find common factors and multiples of two and three numbers

⚡ Add and subtract fractions, including mixed numbers

⚡ Multiply a fraction by a fraction

⚡ Read and plot coordinates in four quadrants

⚡ Plot translations and reflections in four quadrants

I made mistakes, but I tried everything and learnt lots!

Now you are ready for the next books!

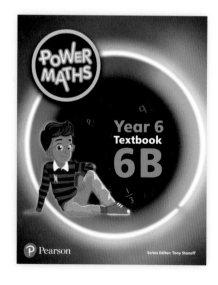

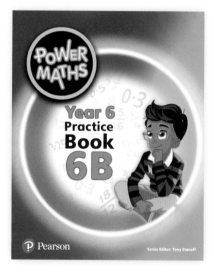